Hospitality

—IN THE SPIRIT OF LOVE

Hospitality

—IN THE SPIRIT OF LOVE

by Peggy Simpson

QUALITY PUBLICATIONS
P.O. BOX 1060 ABILENE, TEXAS 79604

ISBN 0-89137-416-7

DEDICATION

To John, Jeff and Chuck
Your love has made my joy complete.

Table of Contents

Written by Peggy Simpson

Edited by Linda Stanley

Cover art by Susan Wilson

Hospitality: What's It All About?

Most of us think of hospitality in terms of eating together and having fellowship. This idea is limiting, for hospitality is ever so much more than having a meal together. Below I have listed some words describing hospitality. Notice the words which bring to mind the relationship between husband and wife and/or parents and children. Others suggest a correlation with friends, neighbors and the community as a whole as well as strangers.

cordial	courteous	open
friendly	good cheer	companionship
good fellowship	entertainment	welcome
salute	sharing	warm handshake
embrace	hug	take in
to encourage	kind	helpful
sympathetic	neighborly	sociable
peaceful	loving	warm-hearted
attentive	benelovent	accommodating
pleasant	tender	loyal
good-natured	congenial	generous
to amuse	please	interest
enliven	delight	divert
inspire	stimulate	satisfy
humor	relax	make merry
to comfort		

This is not by any means an exhaustive list of words pertaining to hospitality. We will take just a few of these words and talk more about them and what they have to do with hospitality.

Let's talk first about being kind and courteous to one another and being helpful. I think we can group these three together and still get their full meaning.

As I was struggling to get on the train, obviously overburdened by two tired toddlers and a suitcase, an elderly gentleman stepped up to me and asked, "Which do I carry—the boys or the suitcase?" Without a moment's hesitation I gladly accepted his offer of help. Had he asked the ordinary "May I help?", I would probably have foolishly insisted, "No, I can manage, thank you." This happened many years ago, and those two tired toddlers are now two adults. But I have thought about that man's approach to being helpful so many times. We need to develop the attitude of offering specific help rather than the "let me know if I can help" idea. I dare say that none of us really expects to hear anyone say, "Yes, I do need you to come back tomorrow afternoon and keep the children while I go to the doctor." It takes just a little more thought and effort and sometimes a lot more energy when we dare to be positive in our offer and genuine in our concern.

Courtesy and common kindness should begin at home to help develop a strong family framework.

If we practice being nice to each other and to our children, then they will have fewer problems in other homes and among strangers. When we practice true hospitality within our own families, then the results are sure to overflow into the community to include friends and strangers. There is not a single person who, if Jesus knocked at our door in freezing weather and asked for a warm coat, would not give Him the best we had; or, if He should ask to spend the night because He didn't make a reservation ahead of time at the Holiday Inn, would not give Him our own bed if that was the best one in our house. If He should ask for food or simply wish to come in and visit and study with us, which of us wouldn't cook the best cut of meat we could find and certainly be thrilled beyond words to be able to sit down and visit and study with Him.

Matthew 25:40 reminds us: "I tell you the truth, whatever

you did for one of the least of these brothers of mine, you did for me."

God will judge us in accordance with our reaction to human need. He will not ask us even once how much knowledge we have acquired, how much fame we have claimed or what wealth we have gained but simply about the help we have given each other (1 Peter 4:7-11).

The most amazing thing about Jesus's parable in Matthew 25 is the simplicity involved in it. He tells us to help each other in such simple ways as giving a hungry person something to eat, offering the thirsty a drink, welcoming the stranger, cheering the sick and visiting those in jail or prison. These are things anyone can do. They require no special talent, or that we give away our hard-earned money. It is simply giving help to people we meet every day.

The help we give must be uncalculated. We must help people without stopping to think, because we can not pile up eternal merit in a calculated way. It must become a natural, impulsive, quiet reaction of the heart. Notice the attitude of those who failed to help. "If we had known it was you, Lord, we would have gladly helped. But we thought it was some common no-good, not worthy of help."

There are plenty of people who will give, or help, or accommodate in some way if publicity is to follow. This is not the kind of help Christ demands. Jesus is teaching the wonderful truth that the help we withhold from our fellowman we are also withholding from Christ, but if we willingly help one another then we are helping Christ.

How can this be? We know if we really wish to delight a parent's heart all we have to do is help his child. God is the Great Father. The way to delight the heart of God is to help His children—our fellow man. When we learn the generosity which without calculation helps men in the simplest things, we too will know the joy of helping Jesus Christ.

Jesus sometimes knocks on our door in the form of interested people searching earnestly for the truth. I knew of a lady with the Jehovah's Witness church who knocked on more than two hundred doors in an area where the population was mostly Christians. She was turned away at every door with, "We are not interested." Finally she knocked on a door where the lady of the house invited her in and asked if a study could be arranged and the Bible be used as the guide for that study. The Jehovah's Witness lady was converted and is now using that same zeal and enthusiasm for the Lord's church.

Jesus may appear at our door as a child looking for someone to show a little love and concern. He may knock on our door in the form of friends of our children, visitors at church, a troubled friend, a lonely person or a new bride wishing someone would show a little interest in her new and sometimes difficult life.

Almost anything in the world can be bought with money—except the warm impulses of the human heart. They have to be given, and they are priceless in their power to purchase happiness for two people—the recipient and the giver. Many people are timid and afraid of giving of themselves. Perhaps they are afraid of being laughed at, or they may say, "I have nothing of any importance to give anyone." However, while we may think what we have is of no value, it may be just what is needed to fill a great need in someone's life. And if it does that, even for a minute, it will add much to making this world a better place.

There are hundreds of ways to give of yourself. But they have to have their beginning in your heart. Otherwise, they are no better than the rich man who rides along in the comfort of his limousine and throws a penny to the little dirty, barefooted begger child.

To give of yourself you need not worry for a second about your lack of money or material things. You can give extravagantly without reaching once for your pocket book. Of all the things a person can give, money is probably the least permanent in the pleasure it produces.

If you are trying to think of ways to give pleasure to someone—simply stop and think of what brings **you** the most pleasure.

Guaranteed to bring joy to another is a sincere compliment on one's home or children, a note written to let them know you are thinking of them, a cheerful telephone call. Take time to listen to a child, show genuine friendship to a new person on the job, stop to render aid, overlook a slight, practice good sportsmanship.

Extend yourself further by preparing a good meal for your family, being kind to a new student at school, visiting someone who is ill, giving a hand to a person carying a load, aiding the blind, writing a letter to your congressman, or teaching a Bible class or visiting the prison or jail.

Showing hospitality is visiting the sick room, giving a stalled car a push, fishing with your dad, shopping with an aged person, writing to a friend, thinking about God. It is giving financial aid to a needy relative, attending P.T.A., taking an orphan to a football game or movie, calling to say hello to an old friend, handing someone a tract to introduce them to the Lord, checking a widow's needs.

Hospitality is performing every day's job well, thanking your husband or wife for his/her love and devotion, rejoicing over your children's progress, stopping to explain "why" to a teenager, working with your daughter to solve a school problem, a husband taking an evening out to have a special date with his wife, visiting an absentee from worship, building a better neighborhood.

"Then the righteous shall answer Him, 'Lord, when did we see thee hungry and feed thee, or thirsty and give thee drink? And when did we see thee a stranger and welcome thee, or naked and clothe thee? And when did we see thee sick or in prison and visit thee?' And the King will answer them, 'Truly, I say to you, as you did it to one of the least of these my brothers, you did it to me' " (Matthew 25:37-40).

And because our youngest son has just left the nest to complete his education, I would like to add—write a note of encouragement to a young person away from home for the first time.

Can you imagine what it would be like to suddenly wake up one morning and find yourself somewhere other than where you live every day? Suppose you were somewhere far back in the mountains with no telephone, no newspaper, no mail, no people. Just yourself. Well, I can imagine that I might enjoy that atmosphere for a short time. I love the mountains, so it wouldn't be the place that would make me become restless after a short time. I would not like being alone. We all need people, and people need us. I love the song, "People Who Need People are the Luckiest People in the World." God did not make us to just enjoy His world and have a good time. He made us to be companions to other people and to work in His world. Notice Genesis 2:18 and 2:15. It is in the sharing with Him of His continued creation that we add real meaning to our lives. When we cease to be involved in the creative work of God, we soon die.

You remember that Jesus condemned the fig tree to death because it produced no fruit (Matthew 21:19; 24:32; Luke 21-29). Some people seem shocked that Christ would use His power for destructive purposes. But this is the basic law of life. When we cease to bear fruit, we die. If we fail to share with one another of whatever is needed, we are no better than the fig tree which was professing to be something it was not. Profession without practice is a common fault from time to time, but it will do us great harm if we fail to recognize it. Uselessness invites danger.

During his early days in South Africa Mahatma Gandhi inquired into Christianity. After attending a "Christian" church for several weeks, he said, "The congregation did not strike me as being religious and they did not seem devout, but rather, appeared to be worldly-minded people going to church for recreation and in conformity to custom." Therefore, he concluded that there was nothing in Christianity which he did not already possess. Gandi was lost to the Christian World with incalculable consequences to India and to the world.

I believe, truly, that there is one major factor that keeps us from impulsive hospitality, or doing whatever is needed for someone else without thinking. That factor is fear. We are afraid that what we say or do isn't important and couldn't possibly help anybody. We feel we have so little to give that nobody wants it. We are afraid whatever we do will make us nervous. We are afraid we will have to get too involved. We are afraid that if we do this one thing, there will be no end to it. We are afraid it will interfere too much with our own personal life. We are afraid.

You recall when Israel was bordering the Promised Land. They appointed a committee to spy out the land. They found it to be everything God had promised. It literally flowed with the good life of milk and honey, and they wanted very much to possess it. The majority, however, were afraid. They saw giants that made them look like grasshoppers.

We have giants in our lives. Some of them are real and some are imagained. But whether these giants are real or not, the trouble comes when we let them make grasshoppers out of us. Instead of doing what we can, we do nothing because that giant (fear) has overpowered us. Our giant may be some physical problem; it may be time; it may be self-pity; it may be indifference; it may be loneliness; it may be a harmful habit; it may be one of many things. We cannot always make our giants go away, but we must not let them keep us from doing the Lord's work. Many people face giants every day and overcome them. You can too!

Cy Young, perhaps the greatest pitcher of all time, accumulated 511 victories, a mark that has never been threatened. But what is generally forgotten is that Young actually lost almost as many games as he won.

A man with the greatest track record for failures was Thomas A. Edison. He was constantly unsuccessful with many of his experiments. Yet we never think of Thomas Edison as a failure.

Failure is a giant that people would feel a lot less sensitive about if they remembered that failure serves only as a guide-post for one's self.

Sir Walter Scott limped through life on club feet.

Napoleon was an epileptic.

John Milton, who wrote Paradise Lost, was blind as was Homer the Greek Poet.

Louisa May Alcott *(Little Women)* was told she had no talent for writing and to stick with her sewing.

Walt Disney submitted his first drawing and was told to find some other work because he had no talent for drawing.

F. W. Woolworth built a great chain of stores, but when he was 21 he was not allowed to wait on customers in the store where he worked. His employers said he didn't have sense enough to meet the public. He was the janitor.

Josiah Wedgewood whose name stands for lovely china was a lame, uneducated, neglected boy.

Beethoven was deaf.

Before Admiral Richard E. Byrd flew over the North Pole

and the South Pole, he was retired from the United States Navy as unfit for service.

Defeats can be a blessing because they make us more receptive to God. Christ did not come to eliminate the storms or giants of life. He did not come to teach people how to have a good time and avoid trouble. He came to create character. He said to his disciples, "In the world you will have tribulation but be of good cheer; I have overcome the world" (John 16:33).

Through His love and grace we, too, can overcome the giants in our lives and be kind, helpful, considerate and loving of one another.

Something to Think About

1. Assign one of the words pertaining to hospitality to each class member. Have her write a paragraph about that word and its connection with hospitality.
2. Each class member should chose or be assigned a partner. Write a paragraph about that person and the hospitable word that best describes her.
3. During this next week try to be of specific help to someone in your offer of help. This could be for a friend or your family. Report on it next week.
4. What is your pet peeve concerning common courtesy or kindness or lack of it?
5. Look up Proverb 11:25. How does Christ reinforce this statement?
6. Do you have a giant in your daily life? It will help if you will talk about it and share your feelings with others.
7. Keep a diary this week and write down all the positive things you do for others. Share one of these things with the class.

Heart to Heart

"As water reflects a face so a man's heart reflects the man" (Proverbs 27:19).

Could we strike a bargain, you and I? You sit down with that extra cup of tea while I engage you in a bit of conversation (we'll call it thought talk) about whether or not it is really necessary for any of us to be concerned about being hospitable. It may very well be that we are just spinning our wheels thinking that hospitality is demanded of us by the Lord. If the majority of people we know thinks it is foolish and a complete waste of time, energy and money, then they must surely know something we've yet to learn.

After all, why should I practice hospitality? Let's look closely at the teachings of the Lord and find out for ourselves just what He means when He says, "Practice hospitality." Does this only apply to elders and their wives and to people who have large houses and lots of money? Also, we need to find out, not only who, but to whom hospitality should be given.

Was Jesus treated with hospitality while here on earth? According to John 1:10, 11, "He was in the world, and though the world was made through him, the world did not recognize him. He came to that which was his own, but his own did not receive him."

Even from the time of his birth, he was ignored. A great opportunity for ministering was missed by the innkeeper. "And she gave birth to her first born, a son. She wrapped him in strips of cloth and placed him in a manger, because there was no room in the inn" (Luke 2:7).

Opportunities were missed through Jesus' ministry by everyone who knew him. "Jesus replied, 'Foxes have holes and birds of the air have nests, but the Son of Man has no place to lay his head' " (Matthew 8:20).

How then can we be hospitable to Christ? Notice the following scriptures: "Here I am! I stand at the door and knock. If anyone hears my voice and opens the door, I will go in and eat with him and he with me" (Revelation 3:20).

"I tell you the truth, whatever you did for one of the least of these brothers of mine, you did for me" (Matthew 25:40).

"If anyone loves me, he will obey my teaching. My Father will love him, and we will come to him and make our home with him . . . these words are not my own but belong to my Father who sent me" (John 14:23).

The scriptures overflow with teachings on and examples of hospitality. James 2:1-10 teaches that we cannot show hospitality with discrimination. We need to seek those outside our own little circle (Luke 14:15-23).

Romans 12:9-21 gives us the perfect pattern to follow:

> Love must be sincere. Hate what is evil; cling to what is good. Be devoted to one another in brotherly love. Honor one another above yourselves. Never be lacking in zeal, but keep your spiritual fervor, serving the Lord. Be joyful in hope, patient in affliction, faithful in prayer. Share with God's people who are in need. Practice hospitality.
>
> Bless those who persecute you; bless and do not curse. Rejoice with those who rejoice; mourn with those who mourn. Live in harmony with one another. Do not be proud, but be willing to associate with people of low position. Do not be conceited.
>
> Do not repay anyone evil for evil. Be careful to do what is right in the eyes of everybody. If it is possible, as far as it depends on you, live at peace with everyone. Do not take revenge, my friends, but leave room for God's wrath, for it is written: "It is mine to avenge; I will repay," says the Lord. On the contrary: If your enemy is hungry, feed him; If he is thirsty, give him something to drink. In doing this, you will heap burning

coals on his head. Do not be overcome by evil, but overcome evil with good.

God's wrath was used against those who would not receive his people (Deuteronomy 23:3, 4).

Paul points out the peculiar traits to be found in Christians: "Therefore, as God's chosen people, holy and dearly loved, clothe yourselves with compassion, kindness, humility, gentleness and patience. Bear with each other and forgive whatever grievances you may have against one another. Forgive as the Lord forgave you. And over all these virtues put on love, which binds them all together in perfect unity" (Colossians 3:12-14).

Peter reminds us in 1 Peter 4:7-10 that, "The end of all things is near. Therefore be clear minded and self-controlled so that you can pray. Above all, love each other deeply, because love covers over a multitude of sins. Offer hospitality to one another without grumbling. Each one should use whatever gifts he has received to serve others, faithfully administering God's grace in its various forms."

The apostle whom Jesus loved said, "This is how we know what love is: Jesus Christ laid down his life for us. And we ought to lay down our lives for our brothers. If anyone has material possessions and sees his brother in need but has no pity on him, how can the love of God be in him? Dear children, let us not love with words or tongues but with action and in truth. This then is how we know we belong to the truth, and how we set our hearts at rest in his presence whenever our hearts condemn us. For God is greater than our hearts, and He knows everything" (1 John 3:16-20).

Hospitality is commanded. "Be joyful in hope, patient in affliction, faithful in prayer. Share with God's people who are in need. Practice hospitality" (Romans 12:12, 13).

"Offer hospitality to one another without grumbling. Each one should use whatever gift he has received to serve others" (1 Peter 4:9).

Hospitality is required of leaders. "Now the overseer must be above reproach, the husband of but one wife, temperate, self-controlled, respectable, hospitable, able to teach" (1 Timothy 3:2).

"Rather he (the overseer) must be hospitable, one who loves

what is good, who is self-controlled, upright, holy and disciplined" (Titus 1:8).

Hospitality should be shown to strangers. "Do not forget to entertain strangers, for by so doing some people have entertained angels without knowing it" (Hebrews 13:2).

Hospitality should be shown to the poor. "Is it not (God's way) to share your food with the hungry and to provide the poor wanderer with shelter—when you see the naked, to clothe him, and not to turn away from your own flesh and blood?" (Isaiah 58:7).

"But when you give a banquet, invite the poor, the crippled, the lame and the blind and you will be blessed. Although they cannot repay you, you will be repaid at the resurrection of the righteous" (Luke 14:13, 14).

Hospitality should be shown to one's enemies. "Do not kill them, (their enemies), he answered, would you kill men you have captured with your own sword or bow? Set food and water before them so that they may eat and drink and then go back to their master. So he prepared a great feast for them, and after they had finished eating and drinking, he sent them away, and they returned to their master. So the bands from Aram stopped raiding Israel's territory" (2 Kings 6:22, 23).

Says the Lord, "If your enemy is hungry, feed him; if he is thirsty, give him something to drink. In doing this, you will heap burning coals on his head" (Romans 12:20).

Hospitality is an encourager. "You will be blessed (when you feed the poor). Although they cannot repay you, you will be repaid at the resurrection of the righteous" (Luke 14:14).

"Do not forget to entertain strangers, for by so doing some have entertained angels without knowing it. Remember those in prison as if you were their fellow prisoners, and those who are mistreated as if you yourselves were suffering" (Hebrews 13:2, 3).

Bible Men and Women Who Exemplified Hospitality

Melchizadek	Genesis 14:18
Abraham	Genesis 18:3-8
Lot	Genesis 19:2, 3
Laban	Genesis 24:31

Jethro	Exodus 2:20
Manoah	Judges 13:15
Samuel	1 Samuel 9:22
David	2 Samuel 6:19
Barzillai	2 Samuel 19:32
Shunammite	2 Kings 4:8
Nehemiah	Nehemiah 5:17
Job	Job 31:17, 32
Zaccheus	Luke 19:6
Samaritans	John 4:40
Lydia	Acts 16:15
Jason	Acts 17:7
Mnason	Acts 21:16
People of Melitia	Acts 28:2
Publius	Acts 28:7
Gaius	3 John 5-8

Who, then, is to show hospitality? According to these scriptures they fall into three categories: (1) elders and their wives, (2) certain widows and (3) all those who wish to go to heaven!

As Christians we **must** practice hospitality one to another without grumbling! There is no word that describes hospitality better than the word **love.** There is no word that describes love better than the word **give.** The three are synonymous.

Let us open the doors of our hearts today and see how much joy and gladness we can shower onto the world. What purpose is there in hoarding joy, hospitality and love? We cannot leave them to our friends when we die. The only way to be generous with hospitality is to dispense it during our lifetimes. If we let it flow from us every day, its influence will be our precious legacy to our friends and family. Can you think of a better way to be remembered?

Something to Think About

1. According to the scripture, who is to practice hospitality?
2. Name at least five ways we can show hospitality other than sharing meals.
3. What two words best describe hospitality?
4. Do you believe only certain people have the ability to practice hospitality?

5. Name someone specific who has been hospitable to you or a member of your family within the past seven days.
6. Name someone specific to whom you've shown hospitality within the past seven days.
7. Look up the scriptures given on previous pages concerning Bible men and women who exemplified hospitality. Tell how and to whom hospitality was shown.

Coffee, Tea and Compassion

(Colossians 3:12-14 NIV)

During the first century, gatherings were held daily in homes among Christians. This was necessary because there were no church buildings and because the Christians were excited about the opportunity to tell others about the abundant life to be found in Christ. Those people found joy in worshipping, praying and studying together. They were so interested in one another that they were willing to sell their possessions and share with the less fortunate. They shared meals together. Is it any wonder that the Lord added to their number day by day those who were being saved?

In our sometimes cold and unfeeling world, people need and want warmth—the warmth of love and acceptance that can only come through close fellowship and genuine caring. The home is the best place from which these warm qualities can radiate. When a Bible study takes place in the home, it is easier for the learner to relax and feel free to discuss personal doubts and difficulties. The home is the ideal place for genuine communication. It provides the opportunity for sharing the Good News with those who might never learn from a church setting about the promises of Christ and His invitation to a better life.

The Lord knew this when He told us to love one another and show hospitality without grumbling (1 Peter 3:8-12). We must be of one mind, have sympathy with each other and live in brotherly love. We must be compassionate and humble, never returning insult for insult but returning good for bad.

We must demonstrate a humble Christian attitude to those who would take pleasure in seeing us suffer. Throughout the New Testament rings this plea for a right attitude. No one can live the Christian life if his personal life is at odds with his neighbor.

We are to rejoice with those who rejoice and weep with those who weep (Romans 12:15). When one part of our body suffers, we hurt all over. When we really feel good, we feel good all over. It must be the same with Christians who make up the body of Christ (1 Corinthians 12:26). One thing is clear—sympathy, compassion and fellowship do not mix with selfishness. So long as **self** is the most important to us, there is no such thing as sharing without grumbling . . . whether it be sympathy, compassion or hospitality. These virtues depend on the willingness to forget self and identify with the joys or pains of others. There are those who will give of themselves or of their abundance if publicity is to follow, but I believe Christ would say, "They have their reward."

Perhaps a good example of reverse compassion (if there is such a thing) is the time about 17 years ago when we went to visit my sister for the first time after the loss of her husband. Our boys were four and six years old at the time. We had gone just two weeks before for his funeral and had talked much about his massive heart attack and sudden death. We were in the kitchen of my sister's home when she overheard the boys talking in the dining room. The six-year-old said to the four-year-old, "Now Chuck, we must be real careful and not say anything that will make Aunt Bess cry. If you have to ask anything about Uncle Grady, just say, 'Where is Mr. Stewart?' and Aunt Bess won't know who you're talking about and it won't bother her."

This was childish sympathy, but it made my sister laugh and perhaps was just what she needed at that moment.

Compassion is a trait which every hospitable person should possess. In a sense, compassion and pity are in danger of becoming lost virtues. The confused and troubled conditions of today's world tend to dim our eyes and harden our hearts to the needs of others. Too many of us are guilty of drawing a locked circle around our own family and maybe a close friend or two and forgetting that we hold the key. No one gets in, and we are just too busy and too involved with our own acquaintances to care.

We can and do condition our minds to become used to anything. We get used to hearing that there is something in the church that we can do, and we go right on tuning it out and feeling satisfied that being present on Sunday morning is all that is required of us. We get used to hearing about all of the lost souls in the world and completely ignore Mark 16:15, 16. We get used to world conditions and become apathetic to all the calamities we read and hear about. It didn't take us long to get used to hearing the news reports of the long casualty lists each day during the Viet Nam War and to tune them out. We've gotten used to the thousands of refugees wanting to come to America or to some other country where they can be free. We can hear about the John Gacy and Jim Joneses and the corrupt people in high places with little reaction from our hearts, not thinking that each boy killed or cult member who died was somebody's son, daughter, mother or father. It is easy to lose our sense of pity and still easier to feel just a moment of sentimental sorrow and be satisfied that there's nothing we can do.

Pity is the very essence of God, and compassion the very being of Jesus. God's pity was so great that He sent his only Son to die for men, and Jesus's compassion so intense that it took Him to the cross. There can be no Christianity without compassion.

Something to Think About

1. How can selfish concerns cause problems in our relationship with other Christians? With ourselves and God? With ourselves and our neighbors?
2. Read 1 Corinthians 11:17-34; 1 Corinthians 12:4-31; 1 Corinthians 1:11-17. How did selfish concerns cause fellowship problems with the Corinthians? With the Lord's Supper? With spiritual gifts? With baptism?
3. It is compassion in a Christian that makes him want others to know the truth. True/False.
4. When a religious person comes to your door with his/her literature, what is your reaction?

5. If you are not prepared to study with him/her, please try to have a tract with the plan of salvation on hand to give.
6. Think: What if that person is standing next to me at the Judgment and says, "I came to your door and you turned me away."
7. Read Proverb 16:24 and discuss how it fits in with this topic. Also Proverb 15:30 (NIV).
8. Read and discuss the following scriptures: Galatians 5:13; Galatians 6:2; Ephesians 4:2; 1 Thessalonians 5:11; Romans 15:7; Romans 12:10a; Romans 12:10b; 1 Peter 1:22; Romans 13:8; 1 Thessalonians 3:12; 1 John 3:11; 1 John 3:23, 4:7, 11-12; 2 John 5. Please use NIV.

Love Yourself

We talk about doing for others and forgetting self, but truly, one must love one's self before he can love others.

I was riding in a car with a close friend when we came to a busy intersection. We moved to the left turn lane and waited for the light to change. When the arrow came on, my friend turned to me very matter-of-factly and in a very positive way said, **"Don't you just love arrows?"** Feeling sort of dumb I said, "Well, to tell you the truth, I haven't thought about them that much." To which my friend said, "Think about them!" She then explained, "I'm driving along and come to an intersection and stop. All the other traffic stops, too. Then, as if just for me, an arrow comes on. It says to the traffic in three other lanes, 'Stand back, someone very important is coming through' and here I go. I feel just like the Queen of England motoring through while everybody sits and watches."

Everybody is important! Our selves are our most precious possession. We will be judged by our own lives. We are responsible for our own salvation. Others may point the way, but it is up to us to follow their example. We should love ourselves enough to follow good examples.

It is told of Oliver Wendell Holmes that he was strolling along the beach one day near his summer home when he began chatting with a little girl who was playing in the sand. The child soon slipped her hand into his and began walking with him. Before long she said, "I have to go home now."

"Goodbye, my dear" said Dr. Holmes, "and when your mother asks where you've been, tell her you have been walking with Oliver Wendell Holmes."

"And when your folks ask where you have been," said the child, "Tell them you were walking with Mary Susanna Brown."

Love begins with ourselves. In order to love others we must first love ourselves. It would be in good order for us, as we pray private prayers to God, to humbly and gratefully give thanks for ourselves. We should be thankful that God saw reason for our lives and breathed into our souls the breath of life. He knew there were things to be done that only we could do. We should be thankful for our ability to grow and serve. We should be thankful for the spiritual riches that are ours, for our eyes, our ears, and our ability to be able to "take in" the beauty all around. High on that thankful list should be the personal peace and joy that each of us can experience through our dedication to God.

So much of our lives depends on us—upon the realization of our personal worth and potential, upon the development of our skills and talents, and upon our dreams and attitudes toward life.

We can all stand tall in the glory of our unique selfhood. We are fearfully and wonderfully made.

Let us give thanks for all that we are and for all that we are capable of becoming.

Something to Think About

1. Read the 139th Psalm before class. Be prepared to split off into discussion groups and talk about this very personal Psalm.
2. Does David teach us that we should give praise for ourselves?
3. Can you account for the parallel of being thankful for yourself and being hospitable?
4. Try to form the habit of thinking, like David, "When I awake, I am still with you." Wouldn't this be a wonderful thought upon awakening each morning?
5. Notice the way this private Psalm ends. "Search me, O God, and know my heart; test me and know my anxious

thoughts. See if there is any offensive way in me and lead me in the way everlasting.''

6. Pause and have a silent prayer so that you can meditate. Praise God for your life and for knowing you so well. Praise Him for your self and your ability.
7. It is always easy for us to think of our weaknesses and faults, but for a change take a pen and paper and list 10 good qualities about yourself.

Getting to Know You

Meeting and getting to know strangers is not easy. It takes nerve to say, "Why don't you come home with us for dinner?" or "I know you are new in the community. I hope you will enjoy living here, and I want to invite you to worship with us," as you hand them a freshly baked cake.

I wish it were possible to share with you the deep joy my family and I have experienced from the variety of strangers whom we have encountered over the years. These strangers have come from down the street, across town, across the nation and around the world. Some we have met through my husband's work, and others when they have attended worship services with us.

The ability to be hospitable to strangers has to be developed through practice. It is not inborn. Shyness and inhibitions must be overcome. Did you ever stop to think that other people think of you as the stranger and are probably just as shy and insecure as you?

I suppose if there were some way to measure the degree of insecurity and nervousness experienced in the life of any one person, I would surely be far ahead of everyone else. If you could have seen my rating you would surely have said, "She should just crawl in a hole and stay there!" Well, one part of me kept saying that, too, and almost won! But there was another tiny part of me down deep inside that kept saying, "You know that you like people. You **can** overcome your uncertainties if you really want to. You **can** look at more than one person at a time and say something—anything—without your upper lip twitching, or your eyes darting away or your voice quivering. You **can** have company without getting dizzy and having an upset stomach and knots in the esophagus. You **can** invite someone to your house without feeling inferior and apologetic. You **can** invite someone to dinner or for a visit without a memory loss and possible insomnia for the next three or four nights. You **can** make friends with the best of them . . . careful not to choose those who will tend to pull you further down into your weak self."

Whatever your inferior tendencies, I can assure you that I've experienced them and more. Tiny, insignificant and friendly gestures made between myself and anyone else were formerly earthshaking accomplishments. These traits characterized my growing-up years and early adult years. I recall only one teacher in my high school days who showed confidence in me and made me believe that **I** was capable of achieving. To this day I am grateful that Camellia Brantley's life touched mine and that I was a student of hers in home economics. She may not have been aware of her influence. It was her attitude of trust and confidence that came through to me.

By the time I graduated from high school and started working I still did not have very much self-confidence, but somehow (I know now it was through God's wonderful guidance) I managed. I had been able to make a few good friends who believed in me. As time went on my list of friends grew, and I felt that this must be about the most important thing in the world—to have good and true friends of high quality. I still believe this to be a very important and fulfilling part of life.

Then I was most fortunate to find a husband who believed in me more than I ever dreamed possible. He loved me and had complete trust in me. It is still that love, trust and confidence that has kept me believing in myself. I think love, trust and confidence always work two ways. They work together to make family life what it must be if true Christianity is practiced.

So with the help of friends and a good husband, I was able to overcome many problems. My acquaintances always seemed ready to say, "You can do it." After a while, I began to believe them.

I tell you all of this about myself for one reason only—to show that whatever your inadequate feelings are about yourself, you can overcome them if you want to! It is not a simple matter, but you can do it if the desire is there. **Believe in yourself!** As the years went by, my confidence grew to the point that when I took on a project and someone told me verbally or in attitude that it couldn't be done, I worked that much harder to prove that it could! I believe very firmly in Philippians 4:13, "I can do everything through Him who gives me strength." That statement is true, or God wouldn't have put it there!

Now that you and I have gotten better acquainted (at least you know me), I'm ready to share with you a few fun ideas to help you get better acquainted with others. Even if you are shy and timid, if you help people get acquainted and have fun, you will soon realize that you, too, are having fun.

It is easy to slip into the habit of only inviting your very close friends or relatives to your home. Perhaps you could begin getting better acquainted with new contacts by asking them to come for dessert. People love getting together so much that they don't care if they come to dinner or simply for a short visit over cake, cookies, or pie and coffee.

At first you really will have to force yourself. **Don't wait until** (1) the house is ready, (2) the children get older, (3) you are less busy, (4) you get a new spread for the bed in the back bedroom, (5) the kitchen cabinets get painted, or (6) you get new carpet. These are excuses we all use. What we are really saying is, "I'm scared," or "I'll be too nervous," or simply, "I don't want to." Just go ahead. Pick up the telephone and call four people whom you don't know very well and two people with whom you feel very secure. Invite them to come next Friday night around 7:30 or 8:00 to have dessert with you and to visit for a while. Now that you've done that . . . relax . . . and say to yourself, "They **really** are coming; I can hardly wait!" Don't worry about whether or not they'll notice that the front hall has a crack in the ceiling. I can assure you they don't care if the whole ceiling is sagging. Get busy and look through your recipes and decide what you want to serve. The people whom you called are probably more excited than you are, thinking how much they like you and wishing they were as cordial and hospitable as you.

When they arrive on Friday night, invite them in and have them take a seat. Start the conversation by asking about the children, the husbands' or wives' jobs, their hobbies or, if you get desperate, the weather. The idea is simply to get them to talking; then you will probably forget about yourself. In the event you've invited several who are shy, you have your "comfortable" friends there to help you out with the conversation. However, this rarely ever happens. You will find that before you know it, the visit is over and you haven't covered nearly all the subjects you meant to talk about. You will just have to get together again soon . . . to finish!

Well, you did it! Now it wasn't so bad, was it? You may want to try that again next month after hubby gets paid and you can make an extra dessert to have on hand. You remember you saw a new recipe using cake mix and you know the grocery where you shop has them on special tomorrow. You will even find yourself getting excited over who'll be invited next.

The idea is to start on a small scale and work up. Soon you will find that you can invite that stranger at church home with you for Sunday dinner. So what if the breakfast dishes are still in the sink! I'll bet that stranger left dishes in her sink in order to be where she is right now.

Here are a few fun ideas to help you get acquainted or just have fun at your next party. Try them out and then create a few of your own. You'll be amazed and pleased with yourself when you find out that people have been wishing for years that they could come to **your** house because they like being with **you** so much.

"PITCH-IN"

Call some of your favorite people and some you hardly know—perhaps eight in all. Say to them, "Let's have a 'Pitch-In'!" They are sure to say, "What in the world is a 'Pitch-In'?" You will say, "I'm going to pitch in the place for lunch, and you can help pitch in the food." Then tell each one what you want her to bring. You can either plan a menu or have pot-luck salads. Perhaps you will want to furnish the drinks and bread. Set the time and date, and you're all set for a fun day.

When our fellowship group started this, we even suggested that each one bring a small inexpensive gift. The person who has a birthday in the current month gets to select the first gift. The next person to have a birthday is next, etc., until each one selects and opens a gift. This is really fun and a terrific way to get the shy and timid people involved. We usually try to mix the talkative people half and half with very shy people.

The gift idea can really be a source of fun for the whole crowd. Suggest sometimes that each one not spend over one dollar. See just what useful bargains each one can come up with. Monthly themes could be carried out. For example, in February ask each one to bring a **red** gift. It is fun to see what each one selects. In January when everyone is **broke,** suggest that each one bring something out of their house they no longer want like a garage-sale item. Put them all in the middle of the floor, give each guest a handful of beans to represent money and let them bid for the prized possession as you auction them off. Each bean can represent 10 cents. In March an Irish gift would be appropriate. April's gift could have something to do with spring, bunnies or chicks. We do this once a month. Each month someone usually volunteers to be hostess for the next time. We have about five or six "Pitch-In" groups going now and even have people saying, "I want to be in a "Pitch-In" group; it sounds like you all have a barrel of fun!" . . . And, we do!

SPELLING FUN

This idea works best for a group of no less than 20 people and no more than 50. It is a relay game in which two equal lines face each other—perhaps the men against the women. Before their arrival, have large letters cut out from black poster board. Have letters enough to make sure that words which have been pre-chosen can be spelled by both sides. Give each player one letter to hold in front of themselves. When the **word** is called out by the leader, those people holding letters to form that word file out quickly to the end of the line, the men at one end spelling the word and the women spelling it at the other end of the line. Whichever group spells it first, having the letters in front and in the proper order, wins. (This is really more difficult than it sounds and great fun because it is so easy to run to the head of the line and stand there spelling the word, but the letters may not be in order. For example, L O V E may get there first but appear as L E V O). Choose words with three, four or no more than five letters in them. Word suggestions: LOVE, SALE, LOST, BODY, RURAL, GREAT, PASS, MAN, BUG, etc. Each side has to have the same letters. Cut-out letters are usually already available in the church supply room. (Thanks to some friends from the Chisholm Hills Church of Christ for sharing this party idea.)

WHO AM I?

This is a great way to mix your guests so that Jane doesn't always sit next to June, and so that husbands and wives do not sit with one another. When the guests first arrive, instead of having crystal glasses on the table for their beverages, use large waxed-paper cups. Have names of famous people written on the cups which in some way apply to your guests. They will have to figure out which is theirs before they get anything to drink with their meal. Have place cards with that same name already on the table. Guests must find their beverage before sitting down to eat. Example: Peggy Simpson (famous person—Peggy Fleming) or John Simpson (famous person—John Chancellor)

A game along that same line is **Famous Pairs.** Give each male guest the name of the male in a famous couple. Each female should be given the name of the female of a different famous couple. Each must look until they find dinner partners.

I would also like to suggest "Pitch-In" dinners. With the cost of food it really is difficult to have company or extra people for dinner very often. I do not believe that many people are **that** interested in what's for dinner as they are in who's coming to dinner. It is the fellowship that is important. I just cannot say enough about the importance of fellowship and the joys of really getting to know people.

DUNWORKIN' PARTY

This party idea would be especially appropriate for getting retired couples together, for younger people planning a dinner or party for the elderly, or simply to celebrate the completion of a big job such as redecorating.

Some things to do: (1) Let each person tell about his narrowest escape, most memorable Christmas, etc. (2) Play "Stop the Music" (pre-taping bits of familiar tunes) or "Sense of Smell" (prepare small containers of bits of liquid of distinctive odors like witch hazel, wintergreen, Clorax, bay rum, and the like) (3) Sing. Most people enjoy singing.

WATERMELON PARTY

Just for fun have a watermelon cutting when melons are in season. It is a great idea for getting groups together. There is very little work involved since you would probably have the get-together outside. Provide the melons, fork and/or knife, salt and good friends. While everyone is enjoying the cold, juicy and delicious watermelon, call a halt for a little while to have great fun with a **seed squirt** (squeeze the seeds and make them jump). Hold a contest for the best set of false teeth made from the rind or for the most unusual craftsmanship in carving rinds. You may wish to provide a prize to the winner (a box or Cracker Jacks or a lollipop).

HOW TO HAVE A SUCCESSFUL "CHURCH" BRIDAL SHOWER OR TEA
(Without anyone being left holding the short end of the stick)

Choose at least 12 people to serve as hostesses. Each hostess puts in $5, making a total of $60. Choose one hostess to act as chairman (chairmanship rotates). She takes the money and does the ordering and buying. The money pays for cake squares, nuts, punch and flowers. Always make this the standard food to be served. Find someone who makes cake squares, order them and pay for them out of the fund. Usually someone in the group can arrange flowers and if yard flowers are available, use them. If not, order flowers and spend about $10 to $15. There should be $25 to $30 available for the bride's gift. Have a standard gift in mind such as cookware, a serving piece of dinner ware, a toaster, etc. Sign this gift from all of the hostesses. If the bride and/or groom are very special people to any one of the hostesses, she is certainly at liberty to buy them an additional wedding gift if she wishes; but, if not, then the party itself and the hostess gift is a generous gesture by anyone's standards.

If costs go up, you may find that $60 isn't enough; add another hostess or two, but stick with the $5 from each one.

Note: This idea and information was given to me by the ladies at Cox Boulevard Church of Christ, Sheffield, Alabama. This is their standard procedure for bridal teas, **and it works.** I told them that sometimes hostesses like to make trays of party foods themselves. "In that case," they said, "you should not try this party method because then someone would spend more on their party food than someone else, and, generally, after the party is over hostesses end up taking as much home with them as they brought." Their way does indeed work and simplifies the effort for everyone. The friend who gave me the details of this method said that she always likes to volunteer to be a hostess because, "where else can you find a $5 gift?"

Something to Think About

1. How do you feel is the best way to overcome shyness?
2. If you were asked to stand before your ladies' class and make a five minute talk, do you feel that you could do it? The best way to know is to try.
3. Tell of an experience you had when you invited a stranger to your home for a meal.
4. Do you feel that the congregation where you worship is as friendly as it should be? What can you do to make it more so?
5. Look at Genesis 11:6b. Compare this with Philippians 4:13. Do you believe that as long as we do the will of God, **all** things are possible?

6. What is your best idea for really getting to know someone who is now a stranger to you?
7. Do you enjoy having people in your home? If not, why not? Discuss this and perhaps you may be helped to overcome your fears and/or shyness.
8. Discuss Proverbs 18:24.

Have A Good Day!

It seems such a little thing to say to someone in passing, "Have a good day!" But have you ever really thought about how important this statement is? You only have to have one really bad day to appreciate a good day.

What characterizes a good day? Perhaps it is having good things unfold: a friend you haven't heard from in a long time calls, a beautiful flower blooms in your yard, the sun comes out after a long stretch of cold, gloomy weather, an opportunity arises to help someone in need. You have tiptoed into your child's room and watched him in a peaceful and healthful sleep. You are assured by your husband of his love and desire to hurry back home to you after the day's work. Maybe a good day stems from feelings you can't really put into words.

Good health is important. What a blessing it is to start each day feeling good and to have the energy it takes to hop out of bed, stretch, yawn and patter off to the kitchen to start the coffee perking. There are literally thousands with crippling diseases who can never experience this but often awaken in pain or depression.

Setting a goal for yourself and finally achieving it makes for a very good day. Just knowing that you've done your best or hearing someone say, "You've done a good job!" makes your day one of sunshine no matter what the weather is outside.

It is a good day when you realize that you do have the strength of character to overcome a temptation without surrendering. Whether that temptation is big or little . . . the important thing is **you** win! You can turn your back and say, "I will not do that!" It may be saying "no" to a piece of cake when you are trying very hard to stick to a diet, or it may be saying "no" to a flirtatious man who may try to undermine your self respect. It is a good day if we are aware that the goodness of God is always available to us and when we take opportunity to give thanks for our many blessings.

We never know what battles others may be fighting, but it doesn't cost us a cent to pat someone on the back and encourage them with love and friendship by sincerely saying, "Have a good day!"

If you have a good day you have everything! For life and truth and God's blessings come in **One Day Packages**-24 Golden Hours!

Why not start today to form a new habit if you need to by saying to people as you have opportunity, "Have a good day!"

Something to Think About

1. What specific thing makes your day a good day?
2. Read Proverb 12:25 (NIV). Put this into practice today and notice if your day isn't much better.
3. Teacher: Provide your class members with paper and ask each to write down goals to be reached this week. Report next week.
4. Choose prayer partners this week. Always include that person in your prayer each day for the entire week.
5. Teacher: Provide class members with a sheet of note paper, pens and envelopes. Have them write to someone (perhaps a person they haven't talked with in a long while) and tell them something specific they appreciate about that person. Mail it immediately.
6. Whether your congregation fully supports or partially supports one or more missionary families, try to see that each class is assigned one family to care for. Write them a letter at least once a quarter and send them things they need or would like to have occasionally.

Why Don't You Write?

Writing is one of our oldest forms of communicating with another person. It permits one to say what is in his heart, and at the same time it furnishes a tangible record of that conversation.

While the telephone is a marvelous means of communication, it may only bring comfort for the moment. A telephone can be invaluable for calling for immediate answers from across town or for emergencies, but there is nothing quite like a letter. A letter is a part of ourselves on paper, to read and re-read. It is a form of communication that is uniquely our own.

We know how important writing is, for God chose this form of communication to give us his Laws and Promises. He wrote the 10 Commandments on stone tablets (Exodus 24:4). The apostle Paul was a master at writing. He wrote in such a way that his message never sounds as if it were a chore for him. Often he wrote letters to encourage others. Sometimes they had to be written as a form of admonition or discipline, but he nearly always preceded negative comments with encouragement. He encouraged others, although he himself sometimes needed encouragement. This is what makes Paul the marvelous example for us that he is.

For instance, in 2 Timothy 4:9-13 he writes, "Do your best to come to me quickly, for Demas, because he loved this world, has deserted me and has gone to Thessalonica. Crescens has gone to Galatia and Titus to Dalmatia. Only Luke is with me. Get Mark and bring him with you, because he is helpful to me in my ministry. I sent Tychicus to Ephesus. When you come, bring the cloak that I left with Carpus at Troas, and my scrolls, especially the parchments." Notice how important the written word was to Paul. He is saying in effect, "Winter is coming so I need my coat. Please bring it when you come but, above all, don't forget my books—especially my Bible."

There is nothing quite like getting a personal letter, card or note. Fortunately our form of letter writing has changed over the years from the formal, straight-laced, factual correspondence to letters which are casual and only as formal as we are or need to be in a given situation.

Perhaps it would be appropriate to stop right here and tell you what I am trying to do. Here is a book about hospitality, yet this section seems to be offering a course in letter writing. It is because I believe that notes, letters and cards play a very important part in being hospitable. There is nothing quite so rude as to be the recipient of a deed, gift or honor and then to ignore the giver completely. Friendships are sometimes allowed to deteriorate due simply to the lack of written communication.

In wartime, thousands of wives and mothers depended on letters from their husbands and sons to help see them through the ordeal.

You must not say or even think, "But, I don't like to write!" Writing is much like making beds—it becomes a chore only if we want it to. The only stumbling block in letter writing is our attitude. If we think of it as a chore or duty, then that is exactly what it becomes and that is exactly the way our letters will sound.

A good letter is one which reflects our individual personality; even a business letter becomes a reflection of the writer. Unlike the telephone call, putting it all in writing leaves no doubt or question. It gives something to look back on as a lasting record. It is so important that your letter is really **you.** Even the paper we use reflects our moods, our hobbies, our favorite colors, etc. A good letter will sound exactly as if we were carrying on a verbal conversation. Naturalness is the key.

By working to improve your attitude, you can actually enjoy sitting down and putting a visit on paper. If you write a short note try not to make it a duty note (even if it is one), for it will sound just that—a chore or duty. Many times the weather is all that comes to mind to write about, but we can even be happy with that. Be natural and have a positive outlook. . . "Even though it is raining, writing to you makes me feel better!" On birthdays and holidays, "I am thinking of you!" is much more personal than a commercial message and clearly says, "I took the time to tell you that I love you."

Perhaps the fact that you are a poor speller inhibits your attitude toward writing. This need not be! The dictionary can become your inseparable friend. There is even one on the market now for folks like me—*The Poor Spellers' Dictionary.* In most dictionaries you have to know how to spell a word before you can look it up. No more! This one spells the word incorrectly first, or just like you thought it was spelled, then gives the correct spelling right beside it. Isn't that great!!!

Now, here's the part I just love telling you! A letter full of dashes, underlinings and true emotions means ever so much more than the carefully editied, stiff piece that sounds like someone else. We should let go when we write letters. If it's bad news or something unpleasant we need to say, keep in mind **who** will be reading the letter and the sort of person they are. Although honesty is always the best policy, it can be delivered with tact and thoughtfulness. There's no need to get someone more upset than is necessary. We just need to watch what we say when we are having to be the bearer of bad news and say it as well as we can, and maybe use brightly colored stationery rather than a ruled piece of notebook paper. There is no need to edit and work so hard trying to compose a letter to a friend or relative by sticking to the strictest rules of grammar or punctuation. Our very own punctuation can be fun and can say almost as much about us as if we were having a personal visit.

Using three dots . . . can . . . tone . . . down . . . the pace . . . of a . . . letter and give the reader time to pause. . . They can also be used instead of parentheses to isolate a thought. Dashes can speed up letters—put things together—and both dots and dashes are more fun—and just as correct—as colons, semi-colons and periods. They add life to our letters, help our words flow and help out our emotions and moods on paper.

And who doesn't feel excited at the sight of an exclamation mark! Or two!! It makes our letters come alive!!! Although a single question mark indicates a question . . . several make it clear that we are completely bewildered or find something to be totally frustrating. Whoever said that all those strict rules of punctuation and grammar have to apply to a conversation between friends???

One of the rudest examples of a forgotten hospitable act is the absence of a thank you note. There may be those who say that waiting a whole year before you acknowledge a gift is acceptable etiquette, but it is certainly not the Christian thing to do. Who knows? The lepers who were cleansed may have wished a year later or maybe even a month later that they had thanked the Lord, but it was too late. They had had the opportunity to thank Him in person and didn't. If the recipient of a gift does not appreciate it enough to write immediate thanks, then waiting a year is certainly not going to make it any more precious. Thank you notes should never be put off or forgotten.

Even though it may be common to pick up the phone and relay our thanks, it does not replace the written note. A written note always seems to please the giver much more, especially if it contains just a little personality and not just, "Thank you for the gift; I know we will enjoy using it." Don't you agree that with just the tiniest bit of thought that same note could have said, "The blue pillow cases you gave us are beautiful and go so well with both our solid and printed sheets. Thank you for being so thoughtful."

Have you ever thought about a thank you note after a job interview? It is both thoughtful and appropriate, and it will put your name before the employer again. To say, "Thank you for your time and consideration," leaves a good impression of sincerity and responsibility.

One of the hardest letters and/or notes to write is an expression of sympathy. There are many cards printed for this purpose, but again a personal touch means more. It says, "I'm here if you need me. I love you." We don't like to be direct and mention the loss if we can avoid it, but the loss is very real so, even though painful, it is better to say, "Tom's life touched ours and made it richer. His death will leave a void that will long be felt. We loved him." We tend to try to ignore expressing personal feelings by just signing a card. However, I'll be quick to say that signing a card is better than nothing.

Another all too frequently forgotten letter is an invitation. This can be taken care of by phone, but if the person or family lives in another town then a note or letter is a welcome surprise. A note saying, "We would be delighted if you and Joe would join us for dinner next Thursday evening. We will plan for dinner at 6:30 and a long visit following," thrills a 47-year-old woman just as much as a six-year-old child. However, written invitations **do** call for written replies. Three years ago my husband and I got the terrific idea to write to our life-long friends scattered over several states and invite them to dinner. We set the invitation for three months ahead so that arrangements such as vacation time could be made. All who received the invitation accepted. All came except one couple whose son came home following a two-year absence at the exact time on the invitation. We had 28 of our dearest friends show up at our door for an absolutely fantastic evening of reminiscence. We covered everything from high school to college to marriage to babies to P.T.A. to grandchildren (for some), and back.

We just need to be more thoughtful and be specific in our invitations. "Why don't you all come to see us sometime?" doesn't mean a thing in the world. Neither does, "If you are ever in our area be sure and drop by." Be specific with a letter saying, "How about coming to see us on July 17th? We would love for you to spend the night with us, but in any case we want you to come to dinner. Think about it and let us know. We are excited over the possibility of seeing you." Of course, I'm thinking specifically of people who live in other towns or states. But the idea of being specific still holds true and applies to issuing an invitation to anyone, near or far. Inviting someone to **your** home only means that you love that person as much as he or she loves you.

Congratulations seem to mean more when written, as do holiday notes and get-well messages. It is all a matter of being thoughtful and being yourself. Have fun!! Put a part of yourself on the written page. Add color with your paper . . .

bright and splashy or pastel tints, whatever is **you**—but above all . . . write!!! And, with much love.

Something to Think About

1. Write or writing is referred to in the Bible about 60 times. Discuss a few examples of the writers of these scriptures. Moses (Exodus 24:4); God (Exodus 3:18; Deuteronomy 9:10; Jeremiah 30:1-5); John (1 John 2:7, 8; Revelation 19:9).
2. Get a list of recent absentees from the worship service, assign them to class members to write a sincere note of love, telling them that they are missed very much.
3. Get a list of your young people who are away from home either working or in school. Write each one a letter with all the news of home, church and community.
4. Take that same list of young people and do the following: All ladies who would like to participate should make cookies and/or candy. Send a box of goodies to each young person who is away from home (working or at school) for the first time. It will amaze you how grateful they will be and how much it means to them to be remembered. I know of a congregation that does this regularly once or twice a year and it seems to actually strengthen the faith of the recepients while they are away. Just knowing they are kept in the minds of those at home, not only with the packed yummies but also in prayers encourages them.
5. Invite someone to your home this week for a visit and perhaps dessert and coffee. This may be someone you haven't invited before.
6. Make plans for more fellowship among members of your congregation. Plan get-togethers at the church building for Sunday noon and invite all those who may be visiting the worship service that day to stay and eat with you.
7. If you have men or women in the Armed Services from your congregation, try to get a group together to make goodies and yummies for them. When you sent their box, attach a letter also.

Hospitality Begins At Home

Common courtesy and kindness are habits which should be developed within the family framework. If we practice these traits around and with our children, then they will have fewer problems in other homes and among strangers.

There are many ways in which we could make life at home much more enjoyable and interesting while promoting a wholesome, healthy atmosphere. The following questions are addressed to younger members of families, but every one of them apply to parents also. We are all so quick to criticize our children for all the wrong things they do. We need to be just as quick to praise them for the great majority of right things they do. We cannot expect to teach our children the steps to common kindness without walking in them ourselves. Appreciation for a son's efforts, respect for a daughter's privacy, and courtesy to our children's friends are as important for us as parents as for the children.

See how your child scores in the following quiz. If his grade is low, then ask yourself whether you are setting the proper example. Score 10 for each "yes." A grade of 90 or better is excellent; 70 to 80 is good; 60 or below means somebody is in a heap of trouble.

1. Do you always make the effort to tell your mother how good the dinner is or tell your father how nice the yard looks?
2. When something is bothering you, instead of brooding do you go to your parents and ask them to discuss the problem with you?

3. Do you treat your mother with the same respect you would show any other lady by demonstrating the everyday common courtesies for her—opening the door for her, showing her to a seat first, etc.?
4. Do you always respect the privacy due other members of the family? (This includes not listening in on their telephone calls as well as not opening or reading diaries and letters.)
5. Do you make a conscious effort to be pleasant to your parents' friends?
6. Can you honestly say that you have never repeated any important family secrets, even in strictest confidence to your best friend?
7. If you use the family car, before returning it do you clean out the ash trays (if they were used) and remove other trash that seems to accumulate?
8. Do you make an effort to participate enthusiastically when your family has planned some special activity?
9. Do you remember to ask permission in advance before inviting one or more of your friends for a meal?
10. Do you ask permission before borrowing anything from your brother or sister? Do you return it when promised?

After seeing how your children score, it might be well to go right on to a quiz just for parents. These are thought questions I hope parents will seriously consider. Perhaps they will help you take an honest look at yourself and help you see yourself as your children and others see you. Answer true or false.

1. Do I love my children? I never knowingly do anything in their presence which would cause them to be led astray or cause them sorrow.
2. Do I really love my children? I consider their material needs important, but through my actions and example enable them to see that spiritual needs are far more important.
3. Do I really love my children? To the best of my ability I supply the physical needs; but, being older, I can see the total importance of spiritual values. I know with all assurance where I will spend eternity. I want my children to be there with me.
4. Do I really love my children? My children find me at God's house of worship each time the doors are open.

They are with me because I have taught them that love is consistent. They know that I practice what I teach as well as teach what I practice.

5. Do I really love my children? As I make mistakes, my children realize that I am human too. I've never tried to make them believe that I grew up never making mistakes. But when mistakes are made, my children know that neither they nor I should approve of them.
6. Do I really love my children? My children know that I am willing to sacrifice whatever might cause a stumbling block to them so that their way will be easier.
7. Do I really love my children? When I am out among my friends, my conduct is such that nothing would have to change if my children were suddenly present.
8. Do I really love my children? My children will grow up knowing that the best way to show love for the Lord's work is to be involved in the Lord's work.
9. Do I really love my children? My children will grow up with the knowledge that peace, happiness and joy in a home are due to the parents being of one mind and showing accord in the home.
10. Do I really love my children? My chilren never hear negative conversation about the Lord's church, its leaders or members at home.

More than once I have been asked to talk to groups of young people about proper conduct—both in a general way and specifically concerning conduct in worship services. The rest of this section contains information I have written or collected for others along these lines. I think you will agree that the tips given apply to any age, not just to the young.

PEG'S PLATFORM FOR PERFECT POISE
Christian Behavior

1. **Be Congenial** (Romans 12:13). This is the ability to get along with others in a happy way.
2. **Be Dependable** (Isaiah 6:8). This means being trustworthy and reliable. When you make someone a promise, always try to fulfill it.
3. **Be thoughtful** (Proverbs 13:15). Be considerate and

sympathetic. One who is self-centered is usually not a very popular or likeable person.

4. **Be neat.** "Certainly this is a duty, not a sin. Cleanliness is, indeed, next to Godliness" (John Wesley). You are judged by others by the way you look. You never have a second chance to make a good first impression.
5. **Carry yourself well** (Romans 14:4). Poor posture is no mark of distinction. Stooped shoulders, unnatural movements and awkward sitting positions are generally associated with those of low mental caliber and family standing.
6. **Demonstrate good sportsmanship** (Proverbs 29:23). This is the ability to play fair and lose without complaint or win without boasting.
7. **Form good habits** (Proverbs 20:11). Practice these so often that they come naturally. Good home habits will assure good habits in public. It is easier to prevent bad habits than to break them.
8. **Be complimentary** (Proverbs 16:24). Learn to give and receive sincere praise simply and gracefully.
9. **Have strong convictions** (2 Timothy 1:12; Romans 1:16). Convictions are your opinions and firm beliefs about life and how it should be lived.
10. **Take care of your body** (1 Corinthians 3:16). God has entrusted you with his holy temple—your body. To please him you must take proper care of it, treat it reverently and nourish it tenderly.

SIMPLE RULES OF ETIQUETTE
For Young Men

1. Boys should walk on the side next to the street when escorting a young lady.
2. Boys should open the car door for young ladies.
3. Boys should stand ready to assist a young lady in getting out of a car.
4. Boys should open the door for ladies to enter a building, room, etc.
5. At public assemblies, if there is no usher, boys should go in first and locate a seat. If an usher is on duty, the girl follows the usher, then the boy follows her.

6. At a wedding the girl takes the arm of the usher, and the boy follows.
7. Men always rise when a lady enters the room.
8. On stairways men go down in front of ladies, but going up the men follow. This is a safety precaution.

HOW TO MAKE INTRODUCTIONS

1. A man is always introduced to a woman. For example, "Mrs. James this is Mr. Smith." The exception to this rule is that young girls are introduced to older men. "Mr. Jones, this is Mary Smith."
2. A young man is always introduced to an older woman. A young woman is always introduced to an older woman. Exception where the younger person is well known. For example, "Governor Jones, this is my grandfather, Mr. Smith."

Formal Introduction: The word "present" is used. For example, "Professor Jones, may I present Mr. Smith."
Informal Introduction: "Mary, this is Joe Brown. Joe, Mary Thomas."
Acknowledging introductions:
Formal: The correct acknowledgment is simply to say, "How do you do?"
Informal: Young people, you may say "Hello" or "Hi" to other young people but never to older people. That is still, "How do you do?"

HANDSHAKING

1. Men always shake hands with men.
2. A man shakes a lady's hand only when she extends her hand first.
3. Young people seldom shake hands with young people.
4. Close friends seldom shake hands when they meet.
5. Make your hand shake a **firm** and **quick** one.
6. Women never remove gloves to shake hands except to heads of State and other very important people.

CORRECT CHURCH CONDUCT

Why do you attend church? Does this question sound as if I'm completely out of my mind? Whatever your reason might be for going to church, your actions while there act as a showcase and display the real **you** to the entire congregation. They tell your friends how you feel about God, his Word and his works. They also tell what kind of home training you've had. What you think of yourself will also be displayed in your church conduct.

It should go without saying. We attend church (worship) to praise and worship God. It should be just that simple or perhaps that awesome.

The church building is not a gossip session or a place to discuss life. Neither is it a place to air our differences, nor is it a class on how to raise children. It is a place to worship God. If we truly believe this and act accordingly, we will walk in quietly, sit quietly and participate in an orderly manner.

CHECK YOUR CONDUCT

	YES	NO
1. I am regular in my attendance, and I am always on time.	____	____
2. I enter the building prayerfully and with a spirit of reverence.	____	____
3. I always take a seat toward the front and leave the back seats for late comers.	____	____
4. I seat myself in a manner so that people wishing to sit with me won't have to crawl over me.	____	____
5. I try to keep my mind on the service and my thoughts on the Lord.	____	____
6. I know my Bible school lesson ahead of time and do not sit and read it during the worship service.	____	____
7. I try not to time the sermon, and I try to avoid clock watching. (God has given me a whole week; I can certainly give Him my undivided attention for a couple of hours.)	____	____

8. I do not clean my nails nor give manicures in church. This is a sign of disrespect. ____ ____
9. I pay attention to the song leader and start with him on the first word. ____ ____
10. I avoid whispering, note writing, gum chewing, giggling, eating, face powdering and hair combing. These are all signs of immaturity. ____ ____
11. I shun picking at pimples, tussling with the nose and continually coughing. These habits can be distracting and actually nauseating to those around me. ____ ____
12. I try not to do anything that will disturb, distract or annoy those seated around me. ____ ____
13. I close my eyes during prayer and try very hard to keep my mind on what is being said. ____ ____
14. I try to remember not to block the aisles while visiting after the worship service. This can really tire the patience of others and create traffic congestion. ____ ____
15. I never leave the service unless it is absolutely necessary. ____ ____
16. I avoid wearing conspicuous clothes to church. They detract from the effectiveness of the worship service. Loud sport shirts or blouses, strong perfumes, fancy hair-do's should be excluded from the worship service. ____ ____
17. I show high respect for church property. I never carelessly bend or deface a hymnal or write on it. I do not throw paper on the floor. ____ ____
18. I don't prepare to leave during the last song or prayer. This is very distracting to those around me. ____ ____
19. I stay around for a few minutes after the service or class is over. There's no need to rush off. This is the time to get better acquainted. ____ ____
20. I introduce myself to visitors and make them feel welcome. ____ ____

"I was glad when they said unto me, let us go into the house of the Lord" (Psalms 122:1).

With Much Love

In order to prepare our children for this life and the life to come, there is so much we need to teach them in a comparatively short time. But no matter how long and how hard we teach, if we do it without genuine love we are complete failures.

An older woman and her husband walked into a marriage counselor's office and the woman said, "I want you to talk to my daughter. She is newly married and treats her husband terribly." When the husband spoke up and said, "Yes, she really does!" his wife retorted, "Shut up, Henry!"

Do you really wonder where and from whom the daughter learned how to treat a husband?

Ira North says that if a boy really wants to know what sort of woman he is marrying he should take a long look at her mother. The same is true for a girl. A good indication of the kind of person her intended will be is given by observing his father. There are always exceptions, but this is generally true.

Both parents must work hard to teach their children to love. Love **does** have to be learned. In Titus 2:3-5 older women are taught to be reverent in the way they live so that they can teach the younger women to love their husbands and children. Love is not selfish.

We are certainly showing hospitality to our own families when we exhibit our love and understanding to them. If we live right ourselves and not hypocritically, our family will be the first to know. Love is not blind. Love has 20/20 vision.

The eyes of love are wide open—not doubting, suspecting or accusing. Love is trusting and trustworthy. Love is color-blind and sees only the child of God.

Love and praise are the greatest motivating tools we have. When you ask a person who his favorite teacher was and why, he will nearly always answer, "He or she believed in me. I was made to feel that I could do whatever I wanted to do and could achieve any goal." Maybe the words come out a little differently but, if analyzed, would carry this meaning. When love and praise are used sincerely and truthfully, they will not fail (1 Corinthians 13:8).

Love can help us to look beyond the moods and hurt feelings that may flare up between a husband and wife and see the tender moments. We can see through the pouting and shouting that may occur on occasion into a heart that is pure, genuine and compassionate. Love can enable a wife to overlook her husband's forgetfulness of a special occasion and remember the child-like excitement he exhibited when he surprised her with a gift for **no** occasion.

Love looks beyond the dreaded two o'clock feedings into the beautiful face of a sleeping beauty or handsome prince just a little while later.

Love often must act as a disciplining, firm hand to unruly children to enable them to step out into the world and make their mark with confidence and integrity.

Love sees the beautiful bouquet of pansies held up to us by an admiring child and not the muddy footprints left on the remaining plants in a neighbor's flower bed. Love finds a way to explain so that both the neighbor and the child understand.

Love hears a pleading call for help from a neglected, love-starved juvenile instead of seeing a no-account, trouble-making teen-ager.

Love sees through and overcomes intolerence, prejudice and misunderstandings between ourselves and others.

Love sees through discouragements and despair to a ray of hope—a ray that is sometimes only a tiny flicker but becomes stronger and brighter as we believe and work and pray.

Love is not blind. Love sees the goodness in the majority of people. Love has the greatest insight of all virtues and emotions. God is love.

Hospitality has to have its beginning within our own families and has to be practiced . . . WITH MUCH LOVE.

Something to Think About

1. Read 1 Corinthians 13 from the KJV and also from the NIV. Be prepared to discuss this scripture.
2. Do you believe that with our standard of living being what it is today, it is easier or harder for young mothers to teach children the important truths and attitudes that are so needed? Discuss.
3. What place does hospitality have in the husband-wife relationship?
4. What place does hospitality have in the parent-child relationship?
5. Think of an occasion where love was the main factor in bringing forth sound reasoning and rational thinking.
6. Think of an occasion when love proved to be long-suffering.
7. Use several blank pages of paper for "Sharing notes." Write down methods in which love proved to be the best motivating tool.

Shortcuts To Love

Do you agree that when the Lord said, "Love your neighbor as yourself," He meant this in a broad sense? I do! I believe His statements were so profound and yet simple and practical that this particular teaching could cover sharing a much enjoyed recipe just the same as sharing a meal or sharing talents and abilities.

With this view in mind, I have some things to share with you which have proved so very helpful to me. Hopefully, there are tips and suggestions here that will make hospitality easy and a genuine pleasure for you rather than a duty or chore.

There are many ways in which a chore can be turned into a joy. We need only learn to relax, slow down and forget about the hurry-up society around us that keeps beating on our minds saying, "You don't have time!" or "Remember, it costs money to invite extra people in to eat," or "Let someone else do it." Showing hospitality is showing love, and this section is to give you some shortcuts.

Speaking of relaxing and taking shortcuts, I am reminded of something our two boys said several years ago. As I recall, they were about six and eight years old. One evening I started a three week's ironing. I ironed until around 11 p.m. The boys had long since gone to bed. The next morning after my husband had left for work at 7, I got back to the ironing. The boys woke up at 8, got up to use the bathroom, then went back to bed. Then I overheard the younger one say to the older, "Jeff, we might as well get up and cook our own breakfast. Mama has ironed all night."

Perhaps as a starter to making your life happier and more relaxed, we will look at these **Ten Rules For Happier Living:**

Give something away (no strings attached).
Do a kindness (and forget it).
Spend a few minutes with the aged. (Their experience is a priceless guide).
Look intently into the face of a baby (and marvel).
Laugh often (It's life's lubricant).
Give thanks (A thousand times a day is not enough).
Pray (or you will lose the way).
Work (with vim and vigor).
Plan as though you'll live forever (because you will).
Live as though you'll die tomorrow (because you will die on some tomorrow).

—borrowed from an unknown author—

Household Hints:

1. If flower stems are too short when making flower arrangements, insert stems in plastic drinking straws; trim to proper length for your vase.
2. Keep a small magnet in your sewing basket to collect stray straight pins and needles.
3. After dinner, there is usually enough food left for one person. Put in a foil tray or pan, cover with aluminum foil and freeze it. Using a wide tip magic marker, you can write very easily on the foil to label it. After you have several dinners on hand, take them to a shut-in or an elder person who probably has a hard time making it on their limited income. They will only have to heat them before eating. I save them for our sons to take back with them when they are home for the weekend.
4. To remove lime deposits from your teakettle, fill with three parts water and one part vinegar. Bring to a boil and then turn off heat and let stand for a while. Then discard the contents of the kettle and wash.
5. When a recipe calls for sharp cheddar cheese and you have only a mild one, add a bit of pepper, dry mustard and Worcestershire sauce. You will have a sharp cheddar cheese flavor.

6. On days when your children seem particularly bad, try putting lighted candles on the table at supper time. It works magic. Try it and you'll find out that it makes a complete change in their behavior.
7. Watch the dates marked on perishables such as cheese in the grocery. When their expiration date nears, they are likely to be put on sale.
8. Make your shopping list on a long business envelope. Put your grocery coupons that you want to redeem and the food store ads inside. You won't have to backtrack if you make your list to follow the order of the store's goods.
9. Beware of foods at eye-level and arm's reach in the grocery. They are usually the most expensive foods in the store.
10. A quick way to thicken gravy is to use instant potatoes. They blend in easily and thicken the gravy in no time.
11. When taking a bath, always remove the telephone receiver from the hook. If someone calls, they know you're home and will call back. This saves the mad rush to the phone (and a possible accident) only to have the party hang up.
12. Corners cut from used envelopes make great bookmarks. Just slip them over the page you wish to mark.
13. A dish drainer is a handy holder for books and games when a child is ill in bed.
14. For easier shampooing and less waste in the tub and shower, transfer your shampoo to a squeeze-top nozzle bottle.
15. **A Word to the Wife is Sufficient.** Don't be afraid to say, "I'm sorry," and "I love you." These are magic words and need to be used often along with words of praise and gratitude to your husband. Believe in your husband and tell him so.
16. Try never to live your life for the children. It is not a compliment to be able to say that you are a better mother than a wife. You can be both, but be a wife first.
17. Find ways to please your husband. Plan little surprises. This keeps the marriage interesting.
18. Try not to make money so all important in your marriage. I know it is very hard sometimes to make ends meet, but there are times when I believe couples have set up too expensive ends so that the present income will not allow

them to meet. This is often found to be the number one problem in the home.

19. Husbands much prefer a wife in a good frame of mind dressed in a pretty feminine nightgown to a grouch with a spotless and germ-free house.
20. Men should learn not to argue with women who are emotionally upset, for they are unable to reason clearly.

Tips Worth Sharing

1. Hate to throw out bits of left-over vegetables? Then don't do it! Keep a large plastic bowl with a cover in the freezer. When you have small amounts of vegetables such as limas, carrots, peas or potatoes—put them in the plastic bowl and keep frozen until bowl is full. Then get yourself some stew meat and make a potful of delicious beef stew. I use the left-over vegetables, meat, onions, potatoes, a large can of V-8 Vegetable Juice and stew seasonings. Try it. You'll love being so frugal and getting praise for the great stew.
2. When handling hot peppers, either fresh or canned, wear rubber gloves.
3. Use a hollowed-out green pepper as a colorful, edible "bowl" for your favorite dip.
4. Here's a brand new way to serve cheese. Cut cheese into small cubes and insert a pretzel stick. This is much more attractive than toothpicks, and you can eat the whole thing.
5. Use a small nail brush to remove silks from corn on the cob. Use one that's firm enough to grip the silk, yet soft enough not to bruise the corn.
6. When traveling, take a plug-in night light with you. It's much easier to find the bathroom or telephone in an unfamiliar place in the middle of the night. This is especially helpful when traveling with children or an older person.
7. Start fires in your fireplace more easily. Stuff empty waxed paper milk cartons with newspaper. Poke holes in the sides of the carton. Place under wood and ignite.
8. Soften winter-chapped hands with the following treatment: Coat hands with Vaseline or moisture cream and put on

rubber gloves. Then wash dishes or do other work for about an hour.

9. **To Tell The Truth Shopping**

   Everything you buy falls into one of these:

   A. Necessity
   B. Would-like
   C. Better-off-without

Don't kid yourself that a would-like is a necessity. As for the better-off-withouts, nothing can so clutter one's closets and one's days.

A woman who came from an humble background took particular delight as a bride in enriching her new life, making it far more elaborate than what she had known as a girl. This took the form of feeling compelled to buy plates for all manner of highly specialized uses. She bought fish plates, plates for serving corn-on-the-cob, plates for artichokes and plates for asparagus. She bought a partitioned plate for deviled eggs and a server for cocktail sausage. One day as she was cleaning her cupboards she thought, "This is stupid!" She realized that she didn't want to spend another minute washing this unnecessary and exorbitant china. Her fancy plates had fallen into the realm of "better-off-withouts." She sold them at a yard sale with almost no regret for the financial loss, because she had learned something important about herself.

Let's Go Grocery Shopping

Please don't grumble about **having** to go to the grocery. Just be thankful that you **can** go.

1. The highest priced hamburger may not be as tasty as the less expensive; furthermore, it is not necessary to buy the best chopped meat for such things as meat loaf or spaghetti sauce.
2. Easy and economical main dishes that your family likes are your aces. Whether they are macaroni and meatballs or barbecued hot dogs, deal them out with a flourish.
3. Buy ahead when good brand-name food is on sale—soup, canned fruit, frozen vegetables, cheese. Take as much as is practical for the storage space you have available and as you can afford.

4. Don't be ashamed to go into a grocery and only buy the advertised specials. You are not under any obligation to buy another thing.
5. Keep notes or mark your cookbooks of party meals or company meals which have brought you compliments. Serve them again and again. You probably will not be serving them to the same people each time.
6. Clip and collect good, economical recipes and hints for food preparation. Magazines are a source for such information. As you read these, mark the ones that apply to you and your family. Use them until they become a habit.
7. Avoid food fads. Most dietetic foods cost more than standard foods, partly because demand has not yet brought prices down. There are no diet demands which can't be met by using regular foods. Fad foods are the most costly.

10 Easy Steps to Setting up a Budget

1. To discover your financial mistakes, you need to know how your money is being spent. To do this, for at least two weeks keep careful records of every dollar your family spends (one month of detailed record-keeping is even better). This should give you a concrete idea of your family's spending habits.
2. Determine how much you have to spend by adding up your total (take-home) monthly income. Figure on a four-week basis. (Extra paychecks, income-tax refunds, overtime pay and the like should not be included in this figure).
3. Determine your current fixed expenses for rent, mortgage, utilities, insurance payments, transportation, groceries and so on.
4. Subtract these expenses from income to find out what you have left over for credit payments and cash purchases.
5. Keep strict records, making them simple but accurate and complete. The key to a good budget is faithful record-keeping since it enables you to know who you have paid and how much you owe. It also helps predict future expenses.
6. Set aside a specific amount each month for unexpected

expenses.

7. Start a savings account as soon as possible if you haven't one already, and treat the account like a bill. Make regular deposits (weekly or monthly).
8. Stop to think before spending your hard-earned money. Consider your needs first, spend only the amount you can afford for "luxuries."
9. You must be willing to make changes in your daily living habits if you wish to change your financial condition.
10. Use credit wisely. Never use it for everyday expenses.

A Substitute for brown sugar

Measure 1 c. white sugar minus 2 T. Add ¼ c. dark molasses and mix. Let stand one hour before using.

Substitute for sweetened condensed milk

1 c. plus 2 T. dry milk. ½ c. warm water, ¾ c. sugar. Place warm water in bowl; add dry milk and mix well. Add sugar, mix until smooth. May set dish of mixture in pan of hot water to dissolve sugar.

Substitute for sour cream

⅔ c. cottage cheese, ¼ c. water, ¼ t. salt, and 1 t. lemon juice.

Put into blender container and blend until free of lumps. If necessary, use rubber spatula to turn cheese from sides of container into center, so blades can get to it. Makes about 1 cup.

This is very good and also very low in calories.

Substitute for powdered sugar

Put granulated sugar in small amounts (about ½ c. at a time) in the blender. Blend until powder. Continue until you get the amount you need.

Economical Buttermilk

1 ⅔ c. dry milk, 3 ¾ c. water, ½ c. fresh buttermilk. Mix dry milk and water. Add fresh buttermilk and stir until smooth. Allow to clabber at room temperature. Then refrigerate.

Quick and Easy Desserts

Slice a bought pound cake into three layers, lengthwise. Mix a box of lemon instant pudding according to package directions. Use ¼ c. on bottom layer, ¼ c. on second layer, then remainder on top of cake and the sides. For an extra bonus, spread whipped topping on the top of cake (on top of lemon layer) and sprinkle with grated lemon rind. You can keep these things on hand (a cake in the freezer and pudding mix on the self) and be ready for drop-in company.

If you were to ask me to name the best and simplest recipe for a party food, one that has brought the most compliments for the least amont of work, I would say:

Orange Blossoms

1 lb. candy orange slices, cut fine
2 (3 oz.) cans flaked coconut
1 can sweetened condensed milk
1 c. pecans, chopped fine
1 t. vanilla
powdered sugar

Combine all ingredients in an oiled pan (except powdered sugar) and mix well. Bake at 275° for about 30 minutes. Remove from oven, and while still hot spoon mixture into bowl of sifted powdered sugar. Roll into balls the size of walnuts and place on waxed paper to cool and dry out. Makes a big bunch and they are delicious.

If you were to ask me for my favorite **Fudge** recipe, one that our friends rave about as much as my family, I would say:

Fabulous Fudge

1. Mix in a heavy 2 qt. saucepan, 2 ¼ c. sugar, ¾ c. evaporated milk, 16 large marshmallows, ¼ c. margarine and ¼ t. salt.
2. Bring to a boil stirring constantly, over medium heat (mixture will be bubbling all over top). Boil and stir 5 minutes more.
3. Stir in until completely melted, a 6 oz. pkg. semi-sweet

chocolate pieces. Stir in 1 c. chopped pecans and 1 t. vanilla. Spread in a buttered pan to cool. When cooled, cut into about 30 pieces.

If you were to ask me to tell you the easiest and best cobbler pie to make, one that builds delicious memories for your children to take with them as they leave home, I would quickly say:

Peach Roll

I know I said pie and then plainly wrote roll, but it is more like cobbler pie or fruit dumpling.

Pastry: 1 ½ c. self rising flour ½ c. milk ½ c. shortening

Melt 1 stick oleo in pan (I use a Pyrex dish) 12x8x2. Set aside. Roll dough in large round. Use 2 c. peaches (or other fruit or berries). If using canned peaches, drain well. Place peaches on dough and roll like jelly roll. Cut in slices ½ to 1 inch thick. Place cut side down in melted oleo. Sprinkle with 1 ½ c. sugar and 2 c. water over slices. Cook in oven 350° until crust is brown. Note: if using apples, sprinkle with cinnamon. I use the canned, pie-sliced apples.

I would also like to tell you about two more desserts that are so very good. They are old fashioned, easy to make and yet, brand new. You don't find those combinations so often any more.

Bread Pudding

2 c. milk
1 loaf french bread (I use the one minus the seeds on top)
4 eggs
2 c. sugar
4 oz. raisins
2 c. fruit cocktail, use syrup
½ lb. oleo
2 t. vanilla

Chop or tear bread into small pieces. Beat eggs, sugar, milk and vanilla until smooth.

Over bread, pour fruit cocktail with syrup and raisins. Mix well. Pour sugar mixture over this. Cut up oleo over all. Pour mixture into 9x11x2" pan or dish and bake for 30-40 minutes at 375°.

Vanilla Sauce

2 c. milk
2 eggs, beaten
2 t. vanilla
1 ½ c. sugar
2 t. cornstarch

Mix eggs, sugar and cornstarch. Add to hot milk and bring to boil. Let cook for 4 minutes, stirring constantly on medium heat. Serve bread pudding in dessert dishes with sauce spooned over.

Sweet Potato Cobbler

3 medium sweet potatoes (do not use canned)
2 sticks oleo
2 c. sugar
1 c. water off potatoes
2 t. vanilla and pastry for one cobbler

Peel and slice potatoes. Cook in water until barely tender. Place half of slices in 11x13" pan or dish. Sprinkle with dash of salt. Pour over this, ½ c. water off potatoes, 1 c. sugar and cut up one stick of oleo. Cover with half of rolled pastry. Cook in 350° oven until lightly browned. Take out of oven and repeat the above process only adding 2 t. vanilla (sprinkled over all). Top with other half of pastry. Cook until brown. This is absolutely delicious and the same process could probably be used with apples or peaches adding a little cinnamon or mace depending on the fruit.

If you were to ask me to tell you about a quick and easy method of making yeast bread that is so good that when the children come home they always say, "Mom, did you make any of **that** bread?" I would tell you:

Easy Yeast Bread

2 c. self-rising flour
¼ c. oil

¼ c. sugar
¾ c. warm water
1 pkg. yeast

Mix all together and beat vigorously. Butter a loaf pan and spoon the mixture into the pan. Let rise about 30 minutes in a warm place. (Cover the top with a clean dish towel for quicker rising). When doubled in bulk, bake at 400° for 10-12 minutes.

While we're on the subject, why not try these two hot breads that will be ready in less than 10 minutes:

Spicy Sugar Loaf

1 (1 lb.) loaf of white bread
¼ c. butter
⅔ c. sugar
1 t. cinnamon
½ c. sifted powdered sugar
1½-2 T. light cream
2 T. finely chopped nuts

Spread bread slices on one side with softened butter; sprinkle with combined sugar and cinnamon. Put back in shape of loaf. If desired, cut in lengthwise halves and tie with string. Wrap loaf securely in foil and heat in moderate oven (375°) for 20-25 mins. Unwrap, cut and remove string. Make glaze with powdered sugar and cream; pour glaze over top and sprinkle with nuts. Makes 10-12 servings. Your family or your guests will say, "Mmmm, what smells so good?"

Orange Sugar Ring

2 (8 oz.) pkgs. refrigerator biscuits
¼ c. butter, melted
2 T. orange juice
½ c. sugar
½ c. brown sugar, packed
1 t. grated orange rind
1 t. nutmeg

Separate biscuits. Combine butter and orange juice. Mix remaining ingredients in separate bowl. Dip biscuits in butter-orange mixture, then in sugar mixture. Stand upright in well-greased 1 ½ qt. ring mold. Bake in very hot oven (450°)

for 12-15 minutes. Turn out on plate. Then turn your family loose and watch out!

Either of these two breads served with a cup of hot chocolate with a marshmallow on top or coffee makes a great duo for a mid-morning or afternoon break.

I really don't think the recipes should stop until I share with you a stand-by recipe for a **main dish** food and a favorite **salad.**

Savory Chicken Pie

½ pound bulk pork sausage
¼ c. margarine
⅓ c. all-purpose flour
¼ t. salt
1/8 t. pepper
1 (13 ¾ oz.) can chicken broth (1 ¾ c.)
⅔ c. milk
2 c. cubed, cooked or leftover chicken
1 (10 oz.) pkg. frozen peas, thawed (could use canned)
Savory Pastry.

In saucepan brown sausage, breaking into pieces; drain on paper toweling. Pour off fat. In same saucepan melt margarine or butter. Blend in flour, salt and pepper. Stir in chicken broth and milk. Cook and stir till thickened and bubbly; cook 1 minute more. Add browned sausage, cubed chicken and thawed or canned peas (if canned peas are used, drain before using); heat through. Place mixture in a six-cup casserole dish. Top with Savory Pastry. Bake for 25-30 minutes at 425°. Serves six.

Savory Pastry

Combine 1 c. sifted all-purpose flour, 1 t. celery seed, ½ t. salt and ½ t. paprika; cut in ⅓ c. shortening. Sprinkle with 2 T. water, a tablespoon at a time, mixing with fork till all flour is moistened and dough clings together. Gather dough together; press into ball. Roll 1/8 inch thick into size to fit casserole. Cut slits across top before baking.

Seven Layer Salad

1 head lettuce, shredded
1 green pepper, diced
1 c. large onion, chopped
1 16 oz. can peas, drained
2 c. mayonnaise
2 T. brown sugar
½ c. shredded cheddar cheese
½ c. crisp bacon bits

Prepare salad in a large bowl. Layer ingredients one at a time as given. Do not toss. Cover and refrigerate for 8 hours or overnight. Serve in salad bowls, making sure each guest digs down deep to get portion of each layer. This salad will keep one or two days if necessary. Makes 8 generous servings.

Finally, one other fabulous cake recipe. Then you will have my cooking secrets, and I can't think of anyone I'd rather share them with than **you!**

Split Personality Cake

(This will cut into small party fingers, It is very rich).

1 two layer yellow cake mix
¾ c. margarine, melted
⅔ c. (5 ⅓ oz.) can evaporated milk
1 c. pecans, chopped
1 pkg. (6 oz.) semi-sweet chocolate pieces
1 bag (14 oz.) caramels

Combine cake mix, margarine and ⅓ c. milk; mix well. Press half of mixture onto botton of 13x9'' pan. Bake at 350° for 5 minutes. Sprinkle combined nuts and chocolate pieces over baked crust. Melt caramels with remaining evaporated milk in saucepan over low heat; Stir frequently until smooth. Spread caramel mixture evenly over nuts and chocolate pieces. Top with remaining cake mix mixture; (I use my hands to place the stiff mixture over layers) press gently. Bake at 350° for 20 minutes. Cool slightly. Cut while warm. Refrigerate.

If you happen to be studying this book as classroom material, now is the perfect time to think ahead and come prepared to the next class with hints and a favorite recipe for sharing. Select a classmate and share a recipe with her. Make a list of workable household tips that you use and give them to your teacher or instructor. Perhaps she can have copies run off for everyone. This will be a good time to recall how some of the women of the Bible such as Dorcas, Mary, Martha, Lydia and others shared with each other and the community. Can you think of others who shared the simple things of life, such as cooking and sewing, yet made a great impact on the lives of others? I shall ever be grateful for hearing Jim Woodruff of Searcy, Arkansas say, "Don't feel guilty if you can't do the things you see preachers and personal workers doing, such as door to door evangelism. If you cook good corn bread, then do exactly that! But don't forget to share it!"

Something to Think About

1. What do you think of this idea? Perhaps you would like to adopt it for your own. There is a ladies' class in a church nearby that, instead of sending flowers or plants to the hospital when a member is ill, sends a box of snack foods for family members to use while they are sitting with the patient. If you've ever had to sit for very long at the hospital then you know that trips to the snack bar can be expensive.
2. In a recent church bulletin from Richmond, Va., some of the members there who had talents such as playing the guitar or painting and perhaps needlework, were willing to teach others from that congregation one night a week in their home free of charge. Don't you think this is a marvelous way of sharing their God-given talents?
3. When a person develops a talent such as teaching others from God's Word or sewing a pretty seam, it needs to be shared. What do you do that someone else would like to learn?
4. Another congregation in our community is fortunate to have a Registered Nurse as one of its members. The senior citizens get together once a month on Sunday night and have a light covered dish supper together. After supper, their nurse friend takes blood pressure and checks pulse and listens to their heartbeat. She doesn't ever

prescribe treatment or medication but she does reassure them (and in certain cases, recommends their seeing a doctor) and at the same time, is sharing her talent and ability with them.

5. Why not use a little time to think of ways you can help improve the loving attitude of your class or congregation by starting a sharing of talents with fellow members? Is not this first century Christianity?
6. We know how medical costs have soared lately; while I was preparing this material, I was told of two congregations in another area with one or two medical doctors as members. These doctors were kind and considerate enough to want to share their knowledge with the congregation. They have set aside four hours, one afternoon a month for free checks and treatment for those of the congregation who are living on very limited incomes. This includes widows whose income is halted from the time the last child is through high school and until she is 65 years old.
7. Discuss these and other ways we can become more considerate of others by sharing.

Becoming A Star

You truly can become a Star! And an important one at that! That may seem a little redundant, because what other kind of star would there be but an important one? Well, we won't go into that. I would like to tell you that in 10 easy lessons you can become a star, but perhaps that might be a little misleading. One thing for sure . . . you have to have a good attitude, an open mind and a willing heart. These are the necessary ingredients in becoming a star. Let's let the apostle Paul tell us all about it. "Do everything without complaining or arguing so that **you may become** blameless and pure, children of God without fault in a crooked and depraved generation, in which **you shine like stars** in the universe" (Philippians 2:14, 15). Isn't that great! If only we can learn to be content and not take issue with everything that is said to us, so that when people think of us they don't automatically think, "Yuk!"

Now, let's go back to verses 1-5 of Philippians 2. Paul says, "If you have any encouragement from being united with Chrsit, if any comfort in His love, if any fellowship with the Spirit, if any tenderness and compassion, then make my joy complete by being one in Spirit and purpose. Do nothing out of selfish ambition or vain conceit, but in humility consider others better than yourselves. Each of you should look not only to your own interest, but also to the interest of others. Your attitude should be the same as that of Jesus Christ. . ." So there we have it! In a word . . . we are back to hospitality. Only, now we can add a few more words to our already growing list of what hospitality is or is not—not selfish, not conceited, humble, thinks highly of others, shows human interest, encourages, is tender, compassionate, loving and demonstrates a good attitude. These are all qualities and virtues seen in the gracious, hospitable person. Again, let me remind you that hospitality is much more than having a meal together.

One of the best tests you can give yourself to see if you are practicing hospitality is to say to yourself when dealing with others, "What would I do if I **knew** it were Jesus:

Asking me to send a note to Mrs. Jones because she has been sick?

Asking me to go visit that young couple who just lost a child to cancer?

Asking me to go visit at the jail where there is a troubled teen-ager?

Asking me to go for at least one afternoon a month to a young mother's home and say, "I'm here to stay with your children while you go out for 2 or 3 hours?"

Asking me to call on that new family who just moved into our neighborhood to see if they would like to have a home Bible study?

Asking me to write a love note to someone who is no longer attending worship services?

Asking me to be more patient with my children and stop expecting them to excel where I failed?

Asking me to try to understand what it means to be a loving and submissive wife?

Asking me to honor my parents now that they are old and need my care?

Asking me to call an elderly person this week and offer to take him or her to town or to the grocery store?

And on and on and on!

This is really what it is all about. "If you help one of the least of these creations of God you have helped me," Chrsit says.

Each one of us has the talent and ability it takes to become this "Shining Star" in God's universe. We only need to think seriously about how many lives we touch everyday and whether or not we were a good influence and whether or not we passed up opportunities to do good.

Each of us, in some small way, can help people change and be better. We touch lives every single day—in our homes, in the community, in school, church, by telephone and by mail. Our touch is felt and it lingers. It tells others who we are and what we think about. This touch is our influence and our attitude.

Artificial, cold self-righteousness is a thorn in the flesh of the owner and also pricks everyone he touches. A **prick** is not what we need. We need the vital, genuine, sincere human touch of what we really are deep down inside—as children of God in a world in which **we shine like stars in the universe.**

Something to Think About

1. Assignment for this week for the **50-year-olds and under.** Choose an elderly person and offer to take her shopping or to the grocery store or both. Be willing to spend the day with him or her. Report next week.
2. Assignment this week to the **over 50** group. Choose a young mother other than one of your own children and offer to keep her children one afternoon for three hours. Report next week.
3. Assignment this week for the **70 and over.** Write a note to a young person and be encouraging. Be complimentary, not preachy. Maybe you could tell of an incident in your own life when you needed encouraging. Report next week.

For Mothers Only

Turn the hearts of the children
to their parents
Turn the hearts of the parents
to their young
Turn the hearts of us all to
one another
Turn the hearts of the people
to the Lord.

The ads, the magazines, the neighbors smother imagination and dilute courage in the home. If there is a fine furniture store in town, then many of the homes will look as if that store's decorator furnished them all. Yet a person's home is a kind of autobiography. In it may be found evidence of his tastes, his imagination, his aspirations.

Although mounting pressures of conformity sometimes make it difficult, we ought to be sure that our homes—since they are bound to tell things about us—tell an accurate story.

There are three things that we should insist upon: (1) that we can be **comfortable** in our surroundings and not feel like guests in our own homes. (Someone told me the other day that her most vivid memory of her childhood was not being allowed in the living room.); (2) that we have in our homes certain **elements of beauty** from which we can draw the daily bread our spirits hunger for. (I have hanging in my home some of my own cross-stitch plus some paintings by local artists.); and (3) that we have **things around that add bloom to**

our lives such as colors that "do something" for us regardless of how they affect others.

You are defending a small but very precious bit of your heritage of American and Christian individuality when you dare to let your home tell the truth and reflect you!

Boy Wanted

> . . . To fill an important position in any capacity. He must be a boy who treats his mother and sister—and every other boy's mother and sister—with respect and does not refer to his father as the "old man."
>
> He need not be especially brilliant at school, but he must be studious and persevering, never cheating in his examinations or passing a problem until he has mastered it.
>
> He must be truthful, prompt, obedient and industrious. He must make his employer's interest his interest and never be afraid of earning more than his wages.
>
> He is wanted everywhere—in the law, in the medical practice, in the counting room and to run great public works. The people who pay big salaries are looking for him.
>
> The people want him for judge in the court, member of congress, senator and for president, and the nicest girl in the world wants him for her husband.
>
> (Author unknown)

In talking to groups of young mothers, I have heard many times that they often get the impression from older women that their own children were just about perfect when they were growing up and **never** caused mother, teacher, playmate or neighbor one bit of trouble.

Well . . . it's like this. After our children grow up I do honestly believe that the Lord helps us to forget some of the things that troubled us so much while they were little and then "climbing up fool's hill" (as my mother called the years between 14-20). But even though we may forget, well-meaning friends may just delight in reminding us of what our children did that they remember so well.

For instance, we recently met some friends whose children

and our boys played together until they moved away about the time the children reached school age. Mind you, that was 17 years ago. But they couldn't wait to tell us something they had remembered all these past years. It seems that my husband said that he hoped he lived to see the day when Jeff and Chuck (our two boys) butted heads and knocked each other out . . . simultaneously! Now I had forgotten that completely (thankfully) and had just as soon our friends had, too, but they had a better memory about the mischievous things our two did than about their own.

After thinking a moment, I remembered what had brought on that reckless statement. Worship service had ended and we were trying very hard to visit for a few minutes before leaving for home. Our two took off running through the building when Chuck, the younger one, hit his head and caused a tremendous knot on his forehead. On the way home we stopped for gasoline. We were driving away when the attendant looked into the back seat and asked, "What's wrong with the boy's head?" While still driving away, my husband said, "He hit it on the Lord's Table!"

The poor attendant is probably still wondering about that. Then, just a little while later, as we were trying to get lunch on the table, the boys were out in the back yard with a large turtle they had caught. Suddenly, we heard a scream; hurrying out to the back yard we found that somehow, Jeff (the older one) had managed to let the turtle bite him all the way through the thumb. We rushed off to the doctor, not knowing what the treatment would be; for when we called him he said, "This is the first time I've ever treated a turtle bite." However, he only had to give a tetanus shot.

It was then that John said, "I hope I live to see . . ."

As we were laughing about those incidents, I was reminded of something that happened much later when one of our boys was in the ninth grade. He had stayed home from school complaining of a stomach virus. At about mid-morning I had to leave on an errand for a little while. When I got back, my son was as pale as he could be and looked as if he had seen a ghost.

I asked, "What on earth is wrong!?" He said he just felt sick.

Inquiring further, I found out that some of the boys at school had called him on the school's pay phone and told him that his name had been called in chapel and that he was wanted in the president's office.

I asked him if he knew why his name had been called. I suggested that perhaps this was the real reason he had stayed home from school. He answered that he had stayed home only because he didn't feel well, but in the very next breath he began confessing everything he had done or been a party to since the first day of school. When he had finished his confessions, I told him that I would simply call the school and find out why his name had been called and for which of these confessed antics he was "wanted."

I called. The principal said he had not called anyone's name. He suggested that perhaps the boys had just wanted to play a prank on my son by calling him.

After hearing this, my son **really** looked sick. Looking paler than he had ever looked he moaned, "Oh, my goodness! Now I've told you everything for nothing!"

Raising children is not easy. This was a most disturbing incident at the time, but over the years it ceases to be very important. I think this is true of most parents. They forget so many things that their children did that caused them to lose sleep. We like to remember only the good times. I kept a diary when our boys were growing up and wrote down so many things that otherwise would have been forgotten.

Perhaps we who have grown children need to take a more active interest in young mothers. It does seem that once we get older and our children are grown, we want nothing more to do with young families. This is in direct violation of God's teaching. Titus 2:3-5 gives instructions to elders to "teach the older women to be reverent in the way they live, not to be slanderers or addicted to much wine, but to teach what is good. Then they can train the younger women to love their husbands and children, to be self-controlled and pure, to be busy at home, to be kind, and to be subject to their husbands, so that no one will malign the word of God."

What is a Mother?

Somewhere between the youthful energy of a teenager and the golden years of a woman's life, there lives a marvelous and loving person known as "Mother." A mother is a curious mixture of patience, kindness, understanding, discipline, industriousness, purity and love.

A mother can be at one and the same time, both "lovelorn counselor" to a heartsick daughter, and "head football coach" to an athletic son.

A mother can sew the tiniest stitch in the material for that dainty party dress, and she is equally experienced in threading through the heaviest traffic with a station wagon. A mother is the only creature on earth who can cry when she's happy, laugh when she's broken-hearted and work when she's feeling ill. A mother is as gentle as a lamb and as strong as a giant. Only a mother can appear so weak and helpless and yet be the same one who put the fruit jar cover on so tight that even Dad can't get it off. A mother has the angelic voice of a member in the celestial choir as she sings "Brahms Lullaby" to a babe held in her arms; yet this same voice can dwarf the sound of an amplifier when she calls her boys for supper. A mother is a picture of helplessness when Dad is near, and a marvel of resourcefulness when she's alone. A mother has the fascinating ability to be almost everywhere at once, and she alone can somehow squeeze an enormous amount of living into an average day. A mother is old-fashioned to her teen-ager, just mom to the third grader, and simply Mama to a little two-year-old sister. But there is no greater thrill in life than to have your grown son point you out to a group of his friends or to all the world and say, "Hey, that's my Mom!"

(Author unknown)

A Father is . . . .

A father is someone who explains how things work to his boys and sees to it that they learn how to keep and maintain those things when something goes wrong.

A father is someone with extra pennies in his pocket just in case someone **has** to have an ice cream cone.

A father is someone who can fix anything that goes wrong . . . everything from an electrical relay system to a blown bicycle tire to a leaky faucet to a son's heart when his long courtship with his favorite girl breaks off.

A father is someone who is very stern when he has to be but doesn't believe it is unmanly to cry if situations arise that tug at his heart.

A father is someone who will go to any length to see that his children are cared for but forbids that they should ever be given "things" instead of his time or because they were lacking in his own childhood. He believes that strong character is formed through perseverance.

A father is someone who is very likely to use strong measures if his boys don't treat their mother with the utmost respect . . . and prays the tenderest words in their behalf when they falter in some way.

A father is someone who never complains, no matter how ill he becomes . . . but faints at the sight of blood if one of the children gets hurt.

A father is someone who goes to work everyday and takes thoughts of you with him.

A father is someone who bluffs his boys into thinking he takes a cold shower in the dead of winter and just about "checks out in horror" when they call his bluff and pour a bucket of cold water over into the shower while he's in it.

A father is someone who teaches his sons by example that one should always give a little more work to his employer than his wages indicate . . . and thinks that honesty and integrity are very important.

A father is someone with a scratchy face but a very soft heart, and someone you can always look up to, no matter how tall you get.

A father is someone you can talk to about any subject . . . whether it is a faulty alternator in the car or how to control your emotions on a date . . . and know that the advice will be right.

A father may not be a big man in stature, but he is 10 feet tall to his boys.

A father is someone you can love for ever and ever.

(written from a collection of letters written home by our two sons and from a college paper one of our sons wrote entitled, "The Person I Most Admire.")

Bound up in these protraits of a mother and a father are all the many problems that we are faced with daily as we rear our children. Parents who say they have or have had no problems raising their children are deceiving themselves. Certainly there are problems in bringing up a family. There are big problems, little problems and middle-sized problems. These problems have to be dealt with. They will not go away.

Recently, a class of young mothers were asked to list in the order of importance the problems that caused the greatest amount of friction in their lives. The number one problem listed was fatigue and the feeling of being pressured.

Problems with the children ran a very close second.

I feel sure that most mothers keep a running list of things that need to be done, things that might get done and things that **must** get done. The problem is deciding what goes on the **must** list. Young mothers are very busy people, running at a break-neck speed down the road to exhaustion.

"I have to get the children to the bus-stop by 7:15 a.m. That means I have to get up at 5:30 a.m., get breakfast, get the children up at 6 a.m. and my husband up by 6:30. Hurry with breakfast, 'did you put on clean socks? Don't forget to brush your teeth. Be sure and gather up all your books. Do you have your pencil? I hope you did all of your homework. Oh, Bobby! Why didn't you tell me yesterday that you had to have 15 different tree leaves for science today! Well, you'll just have to ask your teacher if you can bring them tomorrow! Come on, Susie! We are going to be late and miss the bus! Your hair looks fine. Everybody in the car? There's the bus! Hurry! Whew! We made it!' " And the day has just begun!

Back home in time to see husband off to work, you are faced with bills to be paid, laundry to do, grocery shopping, a casserole to be made for a sick friend, exercise class (Dear Lord, do I have to?). "My annual physical is overdue. There is a new book I would just love to read. The elders have asked us to read the Bible through this year, and I am already 24 chapters behind. I must somehow find time to catch up. And what about our social obligations? We can't expect to have good friends unless we prove ourselves friendly. The Paces have had us over twice lately, and I just know they are waiting for us to invite them over. I must call and set a date—that's all there is to it! Then maybe I'll at least get the kitchen, dining room and living room cleaned up and a meal prepared. Oh, and I'll have to clean the bathroom and put out fresh towels. The income tax is due soon, so I had better set aside some time for that and . . . excuse me . . . the phone is ringing."

Sound familiar? So we are all very busy—anyone can see that. But what does that have to do with friction in your life? Everything!

Sometimes it is at day's end that more friction arises. The President can talk all he wants to about the **National Energy Shortage**, but it does not compare with the shortage of energy a young mother feels in the early evening hours from 6:00 to 9:00! The dinner is over, the table is cleared, the dishes stacked. She is already tired, but she must wash dishes and see that the older children gather around the kitchen table and do their homework assignments. Several dishwashing interruptions later, while the homework gets attention, comes the time to head the troops toward their baths and then bed. Teeth must be brushed, pajamas put on and diapers pinned. Now comes story and prayer time. Finally, after 15 calls from the beds of the little ones with such emergencies as, "Mama, tell Jimmy to give me my pillow!" or, "Mama, didn't you tell me that tonight was my turn to have Fluffy sleep with me?", and, "Mama, I almost forgot, the teacher said if we don't bring our 15 varieties of tree leaves tomorrow, we don't get to go on the field trip!" And on and on it goes until they are finally sound asleep. It is 9:30 p.m., and you are now supposed to shift gears and put away your "Mama" role and exchange it for the "seductive lover-wife" role inside your own bedroom where your husband is waiting. This familiar scene is shared by millions of young mothers.

So . . . we know the problem, but what is the answer? Everything you feel you **have** to do in any given day and do **not** do makes you feel guilty. You must learn to not take on more commitments than you can handle and stop feeling guilty if at the end of the day, there are several things left on that mental list. I believe there are ways to cut down on activities and be less tired in the evenings. Whether or not you are willing to cut down depends on you.

It seems to have become a trap for young mothers to feel they have to be involved in **all** the things the children do, and the children are involved in everything from school activities to social activities to extra-curricular activities such as scouting, sports, cheerleading, band and a hundred other things. Everything children do seems to need supervision and organization. Whatever happened to children being "let-go" for just a few minutes to play on the playground with other children or out in a field somewhere to gather their own "men" for a ball game and play without 15 adults standing around telling them the rules? It seems more of a status symbol than anything else to see that the children **never** have a free minute for doing nothing. They have to be geared and mechanized for "starting" at 7:30 each morning and then move almost mechanically from study to organized activity to the next planned meeting. They "have" to be in this or that club and be in as many extra-curricular activities as they can and as many as mother can manage. The mental and physical strain becomes so great for both parents and children that when night comes the husband is likely to hear, "**I am beat!** Can't we just go to bed and go to sleep?"

Most women will agree that the daily task of running a house can be managed; it is the many accumulating projects that break the back and brain. All of these "things" are waiting in a long line for the attention of the busy mother and prevent her from ever feeling caught up.

The solution, then, is to not over commit yourself. Don't wait until you are 40 to learn to say **no.** There is no greater work in this world than the work within the walls of your own home, and there is no success to compensate for failure in that home.

I recall the time when our boys were the age to join Little League. It seemed to happen quickly. One minute they were content out in the back yard shooting baskets with their basketball, and the next minute they rushed at me and said, "Mama, **everybody's** parents are gathered up at the Helen Keller ball field and you have to go with us 'cause we have to play Little League!"

Since all of this seemed to be an ultimatum, I went. In a matter of minutes the children were out pitching and hitting the ball, but it seemed like hours before the parents were through organizing. We were told how to go about assigning concession stand duty, uniform duty and car pool duty. The children's positions on the team were of grave importance to all the parents. The children would have to practice every afternoon, and mothers were expected to be there with them. Games would be announced a few days later, but they would likely be every other evening for the duration of the season. The "lucky" ones would go on to **All Star!**

I went for about a half-dozen practices and about three games. The team our boys were with may have been the exception, but it was clearly a sport between parents with the children being used as objects of play. I saw mothers completely and absolutely change from proper, serene ladies to "screaming lunies," and I actually saw several mothers all but tear into one another over whose son caused the foul. They were verbally attacking the officials and each other. One mother was banned from coming to another game all year because of her actions.

After our boys were assured that I had nothing against them personally, they understood perfectly that they could play if they wished, but Mama would not be there. When they finished a practice, they could come home and find supper ready and Mama and Papa relaxed and happy.

Consequently, our boys really didn't care all that much about playing organized ball. They soon got the "left-over" boys together and played ball to their hearts content out on the Commons in front of our house. A few times we witnessed fights among them; I suppose they were finding their "pecking order," but mostly they played ball.

I believe even the lower income family can hire a little help once in a while either for one day, a half-day or two or three hours one night a month. To get away from the children once in a while does the young mother more good than a two-hour counseling session. When you think of hired help you immediately think of a full-time maid and you **know** that you can't possibly afford that, so the thought causes more reason for friction. Call the local high school and talk with the school counselor. Ask for a mature, high school junior or senior to do some cleaning and babysitting. Don't say that you're looking for a regular employee. When the person arrives, try her out for a day and see how she handles responsibility. If she is very efficient, offer her a job for one day or one afternoon a week. This worked for me for several years when I could neither afford nor find an adult to work one day a week.

Young mothers need to learn to slow their pace. You can and must learn to resist the temptation to chase after more pleasures, more hobbies, more social entnaglements, and more activities for the children. You must learn to "hold that line" with the strength of a football player. Before you add anything else to your already busy life, ask yourself, "Is it worthy of my time? What can I leave off if this is added? How will it effect my family life?"

Remember, God made you first a wife and second a mother. Try not to get these roles confused so that you find yourself so devoted to your children and their activities that your husband is lost somewhere out in left field. A husband would much rather come home from work and find his wife there waiting in a relaxed mood with a meal cooking than a harried mother who doesn't wind up the day's activities until long past the evening meal time.

Learn to make do with less so that you **can** stay home. Learn to communicate with your husband. Find the time to read the daily paper so that you can talk about something other than the children. If you will do this, you will find that the house you live in will become that peaceful and happy home where you, your husband and the children can build beautiful memories to last a lifetime.

Sometimes women, especially young married women, apply so much pressure to their husbands for "things" that they are plagued with a feeling of defeat. So many newlyweds want from the beginning what it took their parents 20 years to accumulate. This pressure is more than a lot of marriages can take. Someone told me just the other day that he and his wife work six days a week and that they will probably never have any children. The worst of it is, they work opposite shifts. (No wonder they don't plan to have children.) He went on to say that he is having real trouble with high blood pressure and is overweight. When I showed concern for his health, he said, "Oh, we could get by just fine if my wife didn't work. I could even cut down to five days a week and make it, but there are so many "things" Jane wants for the house that we will have to continue this pace for a good while yet." I was reminded of Luke 12:20, "Whose will these things be?"

Money will buy a bed .... but not sleep;
a book............ but not brains;
food.............. but not appetite;
finery............. but not peace;
a house .... but not a home;
medicine .... but not health;
luxuries .... but not contentment;
things .... but not stability.

It is my prayer that you newlyweds and young mothers will think seriously about what is really important and work at it. Be keepers at home and raise your family to love each other and to love God. This is a full-time job.

Something to Think About

1. Describe, in one word, how you think a stranger would sum up your home in one visit.
2. Compare and discuss Proverbs 21:9 and 21:19.
3. List three ways a wife and mother could maintain a peaceful and happy home for the husband and children.
4. Statistics show that the following reasons are the major causes of divorce. Discuss them and think of the best attitude to have in the various situations.
   Religion money children in-laws
   sex choice of friends social

5. Read Proverbs 31:10-31 from at least three translations. Which do you think is the most accurate for today's woman? Discuss.
6. Of what value are homemaking courses in high school? Should girls be required to take them? What do you think of boys taking the same subject?
7. What would be your suggestions to young mothers if asked, "What can I do to make my day less hectic and less busy?"
8. Who do you think lives under the most pressure in today's society, the young husband or the wife? Discuss.

Glad Abouts

Isn't it great to stop the busy flow of thoughts every now and then and think of simple and plain things that we are **Glad About**?

God is so good to help us work out our lives so that we are at peace with ourselves and happy, that the mates we have are just suited to us and nobody else, and that our children turn out reasonably well-adjusted and decent and honest.

There are so many things to be **Glad About!** I took note of a few things in my own life and asked my friends to give me a list of things in their lives that made them happy. It is good to be with a group of people and slip into conversation about things that make us happy or glad. Sometimes (unfortunately) it is even easier to talk about things that make us unhappy or just plain angry. But we will get to that later. Right now we will talk about glad things. Why don't you stop right now and think of three things that you are glad about. Oh, I know, there are those hundred thousand blessings we all have and many times take for granted that we could say that we are glad about—and be perfectly in order by doing so—but let's think of special and simple things like:

I am so glad that I can be a full-time wife and mother and that my husband's income is sufficient and does not have to be supplemented by me.

I am glad that I have Christian friends.

I am glad that my family are all Christians.

I am especially glad to be an American.

Last summer we visited a large city. We saw signs of sin and corruption in abundance. I said several times to my husband, "I'm so glad we live in a small town."

I'm glad to be a member of a congregation of the Lord's people that believes in carrying out the Great Commission. To be mission-minded is to be like Jesus.

I am glad that women's fashions have a lovely, feminine look about them. It is such a joy to see women look like women.

With the gasoline shortage, I am glad that I enjoy walking.

A little five year old boy told me that having a chocolate pie all to himself on his birthday made him the "gladdest."

I love keeping my grandchildren. I am glad they love staying with us. (From a grandmother, of course.)

And from another grandmother, "I am really glad to see my grandchildren when they visit but I am also glad I don't have full responsibility for them."

And one truthful soul said, "I'm glad to see the children and grandchildren come but I'm also glad to see them go!"

From a 23 year old boy, "I'm glad that I have the parents I have as **my** parents."

From a 19 year old girl, "I'm glad I have a steady boyfriend."

And from a steady two-some, "I don't think we are 'in love' yet, but I am glad that we really **like** each other and have the same goals and ideals to work toward."

A 40 year old woman said, "I have several very good friends and I'm glad. I need all the friends I can get."

I am glad we have lots of trees around our home. I recently visited in a state where trees are very scarce.

On a blank sheet of paper list as many things as you can that make you grateful. Try exchanging ideas in class and see how many you come up with.

Complaint Department

I wondered if I should include this part at all, but then I said, "Why not?" Disappointments are a part of life. Probably the greatest disappointments in life come when people let us down.

My husband and I have just about as many people eat meals with us in any given year as there are days in the year. It is unfortunate, but if we have 200 guests in our home during the year and one person is unpleasant, we tend to remember that **one** instead of the 199 who were wonderful guests. However, I really think that we are most fortunate not to have had more disappointments than we have.

In telling two or three incidents that happened to us, it is my desire for you to laugh and be encouraged by them. If you are somewhat new in learning to be hospitable and someone throws cold water on your parade, it **could** make you wish you hadn't tried at all. Please don't think that way. If someone disappoints you, simply pick yourself up, dust yourself off, and start all over again. Chances are they simply didn't know any better.

We had a group of about 16 people coming for dinner one evening. The guest list included a person well known for his abrasive manner. During the meal this man was hammering away on our table with his fork (in between bites) while crucifying someone halfway around the world. Suddenly he came down so hard on our table with his fork that he not only distressed our table but bent the silver fork he was using. He only slowed his conversation long enough to ask, "Where'd you get this tinware?" Then he went right on in his vexatious manner. I rather doubt that he ever gave another thought to what he had said, nor did he care. I knew instantly that though we would go right on entertaining, he would not be invited again to our home. We like to invite people to our home that we can enjoy as well as hope that they appreciate being invited.

Another time we had invited a whole family to dinner, including a person who was visiting in their home for the summer. I had asked them to come at 6:00. The evening they were to come, 6:00 came and went by . . . no guests. We waited until 6:30. My husband said maybe they had gotten the dates mixed up and I should call them. I called. The lady of the house answered the telephone, and I asked if they had forgotten that today they were supposed to eat with us. She said, "Oh, my goodness! I should have called you. They all decided they had rather go to the movie tonight and just took off a while ago. I'll bet we put you out, didn't we? I hope you didn't go to a lot of trouble for us."

I couldn't help but think of Jesus saying, "The banquet is ready, but those I invited did not deserve to come. Go to the street corners and invite to the banquet anyone you find" (Matthew 22:9). And this is just what we did. We called a couple we knew did not get invited out very much because they tended to leave soon after each service at church. Nobody could get to know them very well. Some thought them to be haughty and self-centered, but just the opposite was true. They were shy but very congenial and pleased that we invited them. It seemed to us that after accepting that spur-of-the-moment invitation to come and eat with us, they began to be friendlier and to tarry more to visit with other Christians after the services.

Once we had invited five couples to come for dinner. Two of the couples had been to our house many times while three couples were coming for the first time. When one of the first-timers arrived, the lady stood at the door alone. We opened the door and said, "Hello, where's Harry?" She said, "He decided he had rather watch a golf game on TV tonight." It always takes a few minutes to recover when someone slaps you in the face, but we recovered and said we were sorry he didn't come.

Those are just three bad incidents out of literally hundreds of good times experienced in our home. I still say that, although a person may have his B.S., M.A., or Ph.D., he may still be a dropout when it comes to everyday common courtesy. He may be totally ignorant in the art of etiquette and gratitude.

We will use the remainder of this space to voice our **Pet Peeves.** Everybody has some. We really will not solve any big problems by talking about them, but it will surely make us feel better. It may even help us look closely at ourselves and see if we are guilty of causing some of these annoyances to others. These were gathered together by asking one person or several persons, "What is your **Pet Peeve?**" It did not have to refer to any particular subject. These are some of the answers I received:

My Pet Peeve is.

. . . the discourteous way people (particularly women) drive on shopping center paking lots. They drive like they are demon-possessed, crisscrossing the area and darting backwards into a parking place while someone else is trying to come in on the right lane and park properly.

. . . the way beauticians talk to one another, making private conversation and jokes while one of them is working on **my** hair. It makes me feel as if I'm being used instead of the way I would like to feel . . . special, because I am paying for her services. She should pay attention to me and try to please me.

. . . to call someone to invite them to have dinner with us and have them say, "Are the children invited?" If someone calls and says, "Jane, we would like for you and Joe to come Thursday night and have dinner with us," don't ask, "What about the children?" If they had wanted the children, they would have included them in the invitation. You should not embarrass the hostess or put her in a bad position by asking. Just know that if the hostess wants you to bring the children she will say so. Either accept the invitation or decline, but please don't say, "We can't come because we don't have anyone to keep the children."

. . . people who are habitually late for everything. For

some unknown reason there are people who feel that others are so honored to have them that they should always make their appearance 30 minutes to an hour later than any one else so that all attention will be on them. I would like very much to see dinners, parties, meetings and luncheons start on time and let the "late comer" be the one to be embarrassed.

. . . for all medicines to be put in "child proof" bottles whether there are small children in the home or not. We should be given a choice of the type cap we want on the bottle. It seems to me that strong children and young people have less trouble with those impossible caps than middle-aged and older people have.

. . . for my husband to pout. When he pouts, it worries me for I never know if he is angry with me for some reason or if he is feeling ill. I will usually ask him if he is angry with me or if he is feeling bad, but he doesn't answer me. Sometimes this lasts for days.

. . . for grown-ups and/or children to have and use bad telephone manners.

. . . for my doctor's receptionist to be so crabby all of the time. She acts like the patients are asking for **her** time rather than asking to see the doctor.

. . . for people to hold a grudge. I wish people could realize how much better **they** would feel if they didn't hold a grudge in their heart.

. . . for people to borrow books and forget to return them. We don't ever mind lending books, we just wish we didn't have to keep track of them and have to ask for them to be returned after six months or a year.

. . . for people who obviously do not have a weight problem to incessantly insist that they do whenever they talk with a person who does have a weight problem.

. . . for people to talk about dieting all of the time when it is obvious they do not intend to do anything about it.

. . . for people to be cruel in their remarks to others concerning their weight. The person who has the weight problem knows it; she does not need to be reminded by well-meaning friends.

Most of the pet peeves from men concerned cars, bad drivers unnessary safety devices on cars meant to protect us from drunk drivers when it's the drunk drivers who need attention, the pollution apparatus on cars, high prices, unemployment and their wives spending too much money.

Write down your pet peeves on a sheet of paper and share them with others. You'll be surprised how much better it makes you feel.

A Woman's Petition To God

No matter what age your children are—two days, two months, two years or 20—a petition to God in their behalf is always in order. At this stage of my own life and my children's my constant prayer is for them to choose Christian wives, remain faithful to the Lord's chruch, and for God to keep their hearts pure and tender and their consciences clean so that when they do things that are wrong, they will have the right attitude and say, "I've done wrong, please forgive me."

But if your children are still young, perhaps your petition to God would be more like this:

"Lord, we have two sons to bring up. Help me to perform my task with wisdom, kindness and cheerfulness. Help me to always see them as they are. Please don't let my pride hide their faults and don't let my fears be magnified so that they develop fears and doubtings. Quicken my judgment so that I shall know how to train them to think as children, to be in all things pure and simple.

"We have two boys to bring up. Give me great patience and a long memory. Let me remember the struggles of my own youth so that I may help when I see them struggling as I did. Let me remember the things that made me glad, so that when I get bogged down with the toils of life, I don't forget that a child's laughter is the light of life.

"We have two boys to bring up. Teach me that love understands all things, knows no weakness and tolerates no selfishness. Keep me from weakening our sons through granting them pleasures that end in pain, ease of body that brings sickness of soul, and a vision of life that ends in death. Grant that I may love my sons wisely as well as motherly.

"We have two sons to bring up. May we teach them values, beauty and the rewards of honest work. Give them understanding hearts and hands that are skillful so that they may work out their own happiness.

"We have two sons to bring up. Help us to send them into the world with a mission of service. Strengthen my mind and heart so that I may teach them that each is truly his brother's keeper.

"We have two boys to bring up. Please guide and direct me that I may do this service to the glory of God, the service of my country and to our sons's physical and spiritual happiness."

I have always loved this prayer by General Douglas Mac Arthur.

> Build me a son, O Lord, who will be strong enough to face himself when he is afraid; one who will be proud and unbending in honest defeat, and humble and gentle in victory.
>
> Build me a son whose wishes will not take the place of deeds; a son who will know Thee . . . and that to know himself is the foundation stone of knowledge.
>
> Lead him, I pray, not in the path of ease and comfort, but under the stress and spur of difficulties and challenge. Here let him learn to stand up in the storm; here let him learn compassion for those who fail.
>
> Built me a son whose heart will be clear, whose goal will be high, a son who will master himself before he seeks to master other men, one who will reach into the future, yet never forget the past.
>
> And after all these things are his, add, I pray, enough of a sense of humor, so that he may always be serious, yet never take himself too seriously. Give him humility, so that he may always remember the simplicity of true greatness, the open mind of true wisdom, and the meekness of true strength.
>
> Then, I his father, will dare to whisper, "I have not lived in vain"
>
> (General Douglas MacArthur)

It is to the fathers that the Lord says, ". . . provoke not

your children to wrath: but bring them up in the nurture and admonition of the Lord'' (Ephesians 6:4). But with God's teaching that wives are to be submissive and that husband and wife are **one**—the admonition is to both.

Perhaps we can think of a few ways that parents can provoke their children to anger:

1. **Unfavorable Criticism.** Have you ever heard a father angrily say to a child, ''You are just like that uncle of your mother's!'' (The child knows exactly which no-good uncle he's talking about.) or, ''Why can't you, just once, bring home a report card like your brother's?''
2. **Constant Nagging Criticism.** Someone has illustrated the point this way, ''One may as well think to grow flowers in frost as to think of educating children in cold rebuke and constant criticism.''
3. **Punishment Out of Proportion.** Children are provoked to anger when parents administer ''corporal punishment'' for insignificant misdeeds. One might spank him or send him to his room for tracking mud in, but no TV for a month???
4. **Ignoring Sincere Questions.** In a restaurant the other day I overheard a small boy asking his mother over and over the simple question, ''May I have a milkshake?'' She ignored him coldly and completely. The little fellow finally made a scene in hot, childish anger. The courtesy of a mere reply perhaps could have avoided both the anger and the embarrassing scene.
5. **Backing Down on Your Word.** Children early have a keen sense of fair play. When you make a habit of breaking your promises, you break their trust in you and you offend their understanding of fairness. You don't play fair, and they know it. This applies also for failing to punish a child when you have promised him you will.
6. **Not Allowing Him to Express Himself.** A teacher in a parent education class once wisely advised, ''Don't always let a child have his way, but always let him have his say.'' Self-expression and communication are healthy for anyone. To habitually deny it to a child is provoking him to anger.
7. **Complete Lack of Discipline.** Authorities in child behavior

confirm that all children want discipline, even though they sometimes (and usually) object. This is true whether the discipline is instructive or corrective. When parents consistently let Junior "get by" with misconduct without appropriate punishment, anger may eventually build into destructive wrath. If you don't correct a child, you are saying, "I don't care." A disciplined child is a loved child.

The golden rule is just as golden when applied to disciplining children. "Therefore, all things whatsoever ye would that men should do unto you, do ye even so to them . . ." (Matthew 7:12).

(Most of the above was taken from the Beltline Church Bulletin, Decatur, Alabama and adapted.)

Something Of Ourselves

In whose home do you visit and get the most enjoyment? What is it about that person or persons that makes you glad you were invited? Do you feel that you are that **type** . . . that when friends visit, they always leave feeling good about having been in your home? Let's stop and analyze the qualities we see and experience in that home where the door always seems to be open.

There are several words that are descriptive of that person or that home we love. The first word that comes to my mind is **comfortable.** To be comfortable with someone in their home is a warm feeling. If that atmosphere is not present, you sense it immediately. It is a wonderful compliment to have someone say, "Your home says 'welcome' in every room." Someone told me that her most vivid memory of her growing-up years was not being allowed into her family's living room. Her mother always said, "Don't go in there, I'm keeping that room nice for company." She says however, that she doesn't remember their ever having invited company.

A desirable quality in a hospitable home is an attitude of **joy** or **gladness** on the part of the members. Paul says over and over, "I am glad and rejoice with all of you. So you should be glad and rejoice with me." There are people we love being with, but others that we would rather never spend more than five minutes with unless absolutely necessary. What is the difference? It is attitude! When I am feeling a little down, I have a friend whom I love to call just to hear her say "Hello." Her hellos will brighten the day for anyone. They literally ring with joy and gladness. On the other hand there are those people who with a simple "hello" make you feel lower than the proverbial "sow's belly." The difference reflects their attitudes toward life . . . for if both types were measured for troubles and blessings, they would probably show the same statistics.

We have examples in the Bible of people who after having been with the Lord had a **glow** about them. Paul says in Philippians 2:14, 15, "Do everything without complaining or arguing so that you may become blameless and pure, children of God without fault in a crooked and depraved generation, in which you shine like stars in the universe." Don't you know someone special whose warm glow of true Christianity became star bright as you got to know them better? He or she is what I would call a genuine person—one who has no artificial or masking behavior or speech.

Children need parents who give them a feeling of **security** and **stability**. Adults also look for this quality in their friends. No one likes the feeling of having been betrayed by someone in whom we put our trust. We like to be with people who have demonstrated by their attitudes and actions that they are faithful friends no matter what. Because their home is stable and secure, they are better able to reach out to others. In 3 John 5 we read, "Dear friend, you are faithful in what you are doing for the brothers, even though they are strangers to you." A couple of verses further on John says, "We ought, therefore, (that is, because the works of the faithful are known) to show hospitality. . ."

It is so wonderful to know people who are genuine and stable. We know that if a stranger should show up asking for rest, food or lodging, we could send them to **that** person with all assurance that they would be received. Whether the service is ever needed, we know they would be willing.

One last reflection on your reflection! No matter how much we try to hide our feelings, we really cannot. Our moods come through just like our reflection in a mirror. Our eyes and our manner will always tell on us. Our eyes do indeed reflect our souls. This is the difference in **most people** and **that person,** under whose table you just love to plant your feet. Whether we are receiving guests into our homes, going shopping with a friend, visiting the sick or shut-ins or sitting with children—we always give a part of ourselves. We may be imparting a mood, a look, a smile or a word. It may be a first and lasting impression. So as we greet one another or wave good-bye, let's try to remember that we are giving something of ourselves to everyone we meet. Why not make it something pleasant! You may very well become **that** person we all picture in our mind as one we love to be with.

Something to Think About

1. Discuss different virtues you like to see in other people.
2. Think. Do you feel that **you** are a person others love being with?
3. Find a scripture that describes one of these good qualities.
4. Discuss this modern proverb, "The older we get, the more like ourselves we become" (Virginia Stafford, Washington, D.C.).
5. How do we get to be older and sweeter?
6. Discuss the following Proverbs: 19:22; 31:26; 16:24; and 27:9.

Note: I must thank my niece, Mrs. Barney (Beverly) Gardner of Memphis, Tennessee for suggesting this topic and idea. Beverly is a young wife and mother who has all the qualities of a loving and hospitable friend.

In The Spirit Of Love

> You will find as you look upon your life that the moments that stand out above everything else are the moments when you have done things in the spirit of love.
> (Henry Drummond)

How I wish I'd kept the appointment! She had called me two days before and asked me to meet her for lunch. She had been in some trouble and was having a hard time with drugs and bad company. She was about 18 years old and needed to talk to someone. She feared a jail sentence awaited her if she returned to the city where she had been staying. I said I would be there and looked forward to seeing her. I even wrote on my Daily Reminder Calendar, "**Meet Crissy for lunch, 12:00 p.m., Thursday.**"

Two days later my husband was very sick and stayed home from work. This was most unusual, for he was rarely ever sick. To salve my conscience I try to say that his being home unexpectedly threw me off schedule. The truth is that I forgot the luncheon date and did not meet Crissy at all.

Late that evening, upon discovering my negligence, tears came streaming down my face. I reached for the phone and called her father, but he said that Crissy had not been there and that they hadn't been in touch with her for over a year. I hung up the phone, cried some more and prayed, "Dear Lord, let me have one more chance to reach that girl. She wanted to talk to me, and I forgot. Can you believe that, Lord? I forgot!"

We never had that chance again, but we did learn later where she was. We went to that town to visit her but were too late.

Have you ever visited a young, beautiful person in jail who was about the age of one of your own children? And did you have to talk through a small round opening in the upper half of a huge steel door and ask, "Is there anything I can do for you?"

Many, many times (and especially at night) I wonder in my thoughts to God, "Where is she now? What has happened to her? Is she hungry? Does she have anyone to talk to? Lord, You can see her and hear her. Please touch her heart with your warm and gentle love. Make her know that **You** care. Let her feel your presence and let her thoughts recall good memories of happier days. And just maybe, Lord, she will come home to those who love her. Please help me never to get too busy and too preoccupied to love . . . and to remember.

"And now, Lord, thank you for giving me so many people and so many opportunities to love; but please forgive me when I fail them. Help them to forgive me, and help me to forgive myself."

In McGuffey's Reader there is a story of an old clock that suddenly quit running. The reason was that the clock had counted the number of times it would have to tick in one year . . . 31,536,000 times. This was just too many ticks for the weary clock, and its morale became so low it just stopped. Later someone explained to the clock it was only expected to tick one tick at a time. After reflecting upon this, the clock regained its spirit and began running again.

So it is with us. Trying to live life in a big lump is frightening. All that is necessary is to do what is necessary at the moment.

Psalms 116:12 asks, "What shall I render to the Lord for all his benefits toward me?" Do you ever pose this question to yourself? Let's ponder it now, and perhaps we will come up with some answers. Notice, it is a very personal question, so the first thing we will have to do is apply it to ourselves. What do I do to render a life of service to God? Since I am the one to answer here, I will start by mentioning several things I don't do. It isn't my daily practice to go door-knocking with Bible in hand to evangelize the neighborhood or to make daily visits to the hospital or nursing homes. There is absolutely nothing wrong with these acts of kindness. In fact, I admire those who can and do perform these acts on a regular basis. It's just that I have to find my service in some other way.

First of all, I try to develop a happy, healthy attitude toward my family and friends. You know, you can't get to first base if you are an old grouch with a narrow mind. So I work constantly on my attitude. This is a never-ending job.

A good attitude is most important at home. Most of us can put on a smiling face to the world, but it is our "at home" attitude that tells on us in the end. What good would it do any of us to be out evangelizing while our own children run loose in the streets and our husbands come home every day to a tired, run-down, critical wife? There is nothing sadder to me than to think I might work overtime trying to win strangers while losing my own family. It is true that I know of a husband and wife who put their children in an orphanage in order that they might do mission work. I think that is a case of someone doing "church work" while completely neglecting the Lord's work (1 Timothy 5:8).

God gave women a very special role to fill. He made us first women, next wives and then mothers. It is not really complimentary to hear a woman say, "I'm a better mother than I am a wife." You can be both, but be a wife first. In today's world we hear a constant hue and cry demanding that women be liberated. The liberation of women began with Christianity, and it ends with Christianity. This is brought out beautifully in the following quote from a sermon by Peter Marshall:

> It had its beginning one night nineteen hundred years ago when there came to a woman named Mary a vision and a message from heaven. The daughters of Mary have been respected, revered, remembered and loved, for men have recognized that womanhood is a sacred and noble thing, that women are made from a finer material than are men . . . are more in touch with the angels of God and have the noblest function that life affords.
>
> Wherever Christianity has spread, for nineteen hundred years, men have bowed and adored.

It remained for the twentieth century, in the name of progress, in the name of tolerance, in the name of broadmindedness, in the name of freedom, to pull her down from her throne and try to make her like a man.

She wanted equality. For nineteen hundred years she had not been equal . . . she had been superior. But now, they said, she wanted equality, and in order to obtain it, she had to step down. It is a far, far better thing in the realm of morals to be old-fashioned than to be ultramodern. The world has enough women who know how to hold their cocktails. The world has enough women who know how to be smart. It needs women who are willing to be simple. The world has enough women who know how to be brilliant. It needs women who will be brave. The world has enough women who are popular. It needs more who are pure.

Don't ever feel guilty about being a wife and mother and having to say "no" to a few church programs for a little while. If you've got a family to raise, let someone else do the "church work" for a time while you do the Lord's work . . . rearing your sons and daughters to be Christian men and women. Your time will come.

Her Occupation

One day the census taker called, and wrote down in a book, and so, as I was hanging 'round, I thought I'd take a look. He had our names and ages all, and put down Dad's vocation, and after Mother's name he wrote she had "no occupation."

Why, Mother's up before it's light, and through the work she races. She starts the breakfast, straightens things, and washes all our faces. She packs our lunches, finds our books, of course it keeps her busy; she washes, irons, sweeps and dusts—you'd think she would get dizzy!

She bakes a cake, and maybe pies; she finds some time for sewing. There's mending, making over, too, because we all are growing. Then dinner comes, and dishes next, first one thing, then another, and when our homework bothers us, we say, "Please help me, Mother."

So, she keeps going all the time, and though she's often weary, she never gets real out of sorts; she's always gay and cheery. She keeps so busy every day, and sure needs some vacation; and yet the census man wrote down she had "no occupation!"

(Elsie Duncan Yale in "The Uplift")

I can render a life of service to God by trying to be the woman that God wants me to be and by trying to be the kind of wife that suits my husband and the kind of mother that suits God.

I can render a life of service to God by being hospitable. If you know me at all, then you knew I would say that.

What sort of mental picture do you get when you think of the word hospitality? If you immediately think of a perfect hostess in her beautiful home with perfect children all performing their various jobs to help their mother get the perfect meal on the table for just the "right" guests, then chances are you do not do much entertaining! Most of us will never reach this state of perfection. Someone said to me just the other day that people who have "everything" are never at home to enjoy it. They (husband and wife) work six days a week in order to make the payments on all their "things." You do not have to have everything in order to enjoy people. In fact, just the opposite is generally true.

There are people who will work long hours in order to keep up with the "in" people. Then just when they feel they have reached that materialistic goal and feel ready to say to the Joneses, "Hey look! We have arrived!", they find that the Joneses have refinanced, and are off again!

A few years ago when a group of Christian women were in the early stages of restoring the T. B. Larimore House in Florence, Alabama, my husband, John, and son, Chuck, were asked to go pick up an antique bedroom suite somewhere in Tennessee. It was about a four and a half or five hour trip which put them there right at lunch time. They had planned to load the furniture and have lunch at the nearest McDonalds, but the man in whose home the furniture had been stored would not hear of it! He just insisted that John and Chuck have lunch with them. He said that his wife was preparing lunch right then and that setting two more places was no bother. That day's lunch consisted of a bowl of bean soup and three or four pieces of leftover cornbread split in half so as to have enough to go around. But do you know John and Chuck still remember that warm hospitality, genuine love and friendship when they've forgotten dozens of other meals where great care was taken to impress the guests. Genuine hospitality was shown by kindness and generosity.

When Paul told the Romans to practice hospitality, it included contributing to the saints (Romans 12:13). In Acts 11:27-30, when some brethren came down from Jerusalem to Antioch to tell of the great famine that was coming on all the land of Israel, the believers sent relief to the Christians in Judea, each giving all he could. Is it any wonder that believers were first called Christians in Antioch?

"May the Lord deal kindly with you, as you have dealt with the dead and with me," was the parting message of Naomi to her daughters-in-law, Ruth and Orpah (Ruth 1:8). How few of us would dare ask God at night to deal with us tomorrow as we have dealt with others today. Even if we say we did nothing, how would it be if God did nothing for us! Yet, let us not forget that God **will** deal with us as we have dealt with others.

I can render a life of service to God by encouraging others, especially my husband and children. Whatever good a married Christian man does is strengthened and enlarged by the Christian wife at his side. She is the one who encourages him and makes him believe that he can do great things with God's help. If she does not build his confidence, he is almost surely defeated before he begins. Not many preachers could continue to preach without wives who want them to preach. Not many missionaries are effective on the mission field without the support and devotion of wives who are like-minded. Few men would teach Bible classes if the wife was always critical and discouraging. Elders and deacons do not serve well unless they have wives who are an inspiration to them and to others. A Christian wife serves just as surely as does her husband in every way in which he serves God.

Just as the home can make or break a man, it is also

the training ground of children. If Christianity is to have much impact in our generation, its thrust must come from the home. The God-fearing mother has an influence that reaches into eternity, as her teachings and example are reflected in her children and their children for generations to come. Did you know that 19 out of 20 who become Christians do so before they reach the age of 25? After 25 only one in 10,000 obey God; after 35, one in 50,000; after 45, one in 200,000; after 75, one in 700,000. The emphasis in the Bible is upon teaching our children. It appears that the sooner one becomes a Christian after reaching accountability the better. So I would tell you never to discourage your son or daughter in his desire to become a Christian.

I longed to write a poem of
The rail fence heaped with snow.
Instead, I baked a cherry pie
Because David liked them so.

I longed to paint a picture of
The pear tree, white with bloom.
Instead, I made a braided rug
to brighten Martha's room.

I longed to sing a little song
Ere youth and dreams had flown—
Instead, I bathed Joan's bleeding knee
And smoothed a bandage on.

I'll never do those dreamed of things
I've waited for so long—
Now, David writes, Martha paints,
Joan sings a happy song.

(Author unknown)

We are much too quick to pass out criticisms and judgments on all the wrong things our children do. We should be even quicker to pass out compliments and point out the good things they do. I saw a bumper sticker the other day that said, "Have you hugged your child today?" Why don't you do that very thing right now and, while you're at it, hug your husband, too, and tell him you love him very much. Your day will be better and theirs will be too!

An incident comes to my mind when it was hard to know which emotion to follow, praise or criticism, to something our boys did when they were very young.

It was December and I had allowed them to walk the few blocks to town one day to shop for a Christmas present for their dad. They each had one dollar. They went to the dime store and while one choose a tie, the other choose a golf club tie bar (their father never played golf in his life). They paid for them and then walked across the street to a fine men's shop. When asked, "Can we help you?" the boys asked, "Do you gift wrap?"

"We surely do!" was the man's friendly reply. "What do you need?"

To this, the boys laid their dime store purchases on the counter and said, "We don't want to buy anything but would you please gift wrap these things we've already bought. They told us they didn't gift wrap where we bought them."

The boys brought in gifts, beautifully gift-wrapped, even bearing the sticker from the expensive men's store.

I can render a life of service to God by being grateful. Ingratitude is a sin, and God doesn't like it. Gratitude produces in me a new way to look at myself. I can like myself; and if I like myself, I will like others. God made me and He knows me. He has given me a unique physical appearance, intellect, talent and station in life. I have the hope of eternal life. Learning to be grateful for all the small things in life will help me develop a good healthy attitude toward myself and others.

A few years ago there was a story in *The Reader's Digest* telling of a young man in North Carolina who lost his vision. He was fortunate in that he could have a transplant whenever one became available. Several months later a young lady in another part of the nation died and left her eyes to the Eye Bank so that someone else might see. The young man was notified to be at the hospital within hours of the girl's death to receive the transplant.

While he was recuperating, he was thinking just how fortunate and how thankful he was that soon he would see again. He decided he would write to someone expressing his gratitude. He knew that he couldn't thank the donor's family, because this information is confidential; so he wrote to the

Eye Bank at Boston, Mass., in care of the doctor in charge. The boy wrote, "I am 29 years old, a senior at the University of Tennessee, studying to be an engineer and love to ski and write as hobbies. If you would somehow let the family know that I am coming along just fine and cannot find the words to say just how grateful I am that soon I will see again."

In the years that this doctor had been director of the Eye Bank, more than 5,000 corneas had been shipped to all parts of the country. This was only the second time they had ever received a "thank you."

I can render a life of service to God by learning to be a good listener. Listening is an art and has to be learned. Paul said, "When I am with them whose conscience bothers them easily, I don't act as though I know it all and don't say they are foolish; the result is that they are willing to let me help them. Yes, whatever a person is like, I try to find common ground with him so he will let me teach him about Christ and let Christ save him" (1 Corinthians 9:22, paraphrase).

Listening shows we care. We let God love others through us. We need to be aware of others' needs and try to just listen. Haven't you known people who weren't really listening while you were talking to them but were only waiting for you to pause long enough to allow them to jump in and start talking themselves? If someone knocks at your door with a problem, she doesn't care one bit how your house looks. She needs your sympathetic ear. Don't turn her away with your apologies about the house. The door may be closed on any future talks.

To be available when needed is to be a special instrument for sharing Chrsit. He was the most sympathetic listener and compassionate companion the world has ever known. So if listening is our unique talent, we may plant the seed of Christ while someone else may come along later to cultivate the harvest. We must share Christ with a willingness to listen. We do this by getting involved in other people's lives and being truly concerned. It is not enough that we have the truth . . . we must **be** the truth.

The areas of service I've mentioned may not be what you would consider great by the world's standards, but I believe very firmly that God gave each of us very special and unique roles to fill. If we fill our role to the best of our ability, we won't need to feel guilty about what we didn't do. We are all ordinary—it is Jesus being in our lives that makes us extra-ordinary. Arise! And let us be going! Where do we go? If we lack anything in our lives, then we can go shopping.

I Must Go Shopping

I must go shopping. I am completely out of generosity and I want to get some. I also want to exchange this self-satisfaction that I picked up the other day for some real humility . . . they say it wears better.

I want to look for tolerance—which is worn for a wrap this season. I saw some samples of kindness, and I'm a little low on it right now. One can't get too much of it. I must try to match some patience. I saw it on a friend, and it was so becoming. I must remember to get my sense of humor mended. Yes, I must go shopping today.

Note: Some of these pages under this topic contain ideas and thoughts of many other people. I used pages of notes taken at various workshops and Bible classes. I do not know to whom credit should go for some of the thoughts written here. Generally, when I take notes I do take them verbatim but write them in my own way. However, if **you** see something that you recognize as belonging to you or someone you know, please accept my gratitude and my apologies for someone else's ideas.

Something to Think About

1. What do you feel is your best area of service to God? Discuss.
2. Discuss 1 Timothy 5:8 and also Titus 2:5.
3. What do you think is the major problem in the American home today? Discuss.
4. Do you believe that children get the proper training in Day Care Centers?
5. The word Christian is only used about three times in the entire New Testament. It must carry a tremendous meaning. Do you think we take to too lightly? Look at what the

people did in Acts 11:27-30 to deserve the title.

6. Think of three things that have to do with keeping house and homemaking for which you are thankful. Someone said they were thankful for dirty dishes. This meant they had plenty to eat whereas many millions of people cannot say this.
7. For a goal this week, try to do something for someone each day this week with a spirit of love. Report next week.